Mythical Odes

Across the Ages

A Collection of Lyrical Verses, Choral
Renditions, and Epic Retellings

by
PETA OAKES

(GAELIC MAC DUBHDARA)

Mythical Odes Across the Ages

Copyright © 2024 by Peta Oakes

All Rights Reserved

No part of this book may be reproduced or transmitted in any form or by any means, electronic or mechanical, including photocopying, recording, or by any information storage and retrieval system without the written permission of the author, except where permitted by law.

ISBN: 978-1-917367-75-2

In the timeless embrace of myth and legend, we embark on a journey where love's melodies intertwine with the echoes of eternity.

Acknowledgments

I am profoundly thankful for the rich tapestry of ancient myths and timeless tales that underpin this collection of lyrical verses, facilitating the emergence of a distinctive hybrid poetic form. Their enduring resonance not only inspires but also serves as a guiding beacon for creative exploration.

To my mentors,

your wisdom and encouragement have been invaluable on this journey. Thank you for sharing your insights and nurturing my growth as a writer.

To my daughter,

your support has been my North Star.

Special thanks to the Publisher for launching these lyrical verses into the vast cosmos. Your belief in the power of words is the wind beneath my writer's wings.

Table of Contents

Chapter 1: A Tapestry of Love..2

Chapter 2: Melodies of Eternal Longing........................11

Chapter 3: A Symphony of Transformation 21

Chapter 4: Tragedy in Mulberry Red................................30

Chapter 5: Envy's Dark Whispers......................................39

Chapter 6: A Pomegranate's Pact......................................48

Chapter 7: Golden Fleece of Betrayal 57

Chapter 8: Beauty's Price..66

Chapter 9: A Golden Race of Love 75

Chapter 10: Reflections of Loves Solitude 84

Chapter 11: Cloak of Deceit 93

Chapter 12: Threads of Destiny 102

Chapter 13: Bloom of Eternal Beauty 111

Chapter 14: A Humble Union 120

Chapter 15: A Kingdom in Flames..................................130

Chapter 16: Constellations of Love 139

Chapter 17: Melodic Metamorphosis 149

Chapter 18: A Swim Through Love's Depths................158

Chapter 19: Eternal Spring of Love.................................167

Chapter 20: Firey Celestial Descent.................................176

Conclusion...184

About the Author 186

Chapter 1: A Tapestry of Love

Eros and Psyche: A Lyrical Ode

Prologue

This beautiful ode is a retelling of the myth of Eros (Cupid) and Psyche from Greek mythology.

In the lands of myth and lore,
Where love's mysteries explore,
A tale of passion, rare and true,
Of Eros and Psyche, I sing to you.

In heavens high, their story starts,
Where gods and mortals play their parts.
Eros, with arrows, swift and keen,

Psyche, in beauty, unseen.

Through whispered winds, their love does grow,
In the fields where wildflowers sow.
Eros, the archer, Psyche, so fair,
Their love a flame, beyond compare.

Psyche, mortal, in beauty's grace,
Caught in Eros' warm embrace.
On wings of love, they take their flight,
Bound together in pure delight.

In Cupid's bow, their fate entwined,
A love story, for all time.
Psyche's journey, a mortal's quest,
A testament to love's eternal zest.

Through trials and tests, their love endures,
In celestial realms, it matures.
Eros and Psyche, their tale unfolds,
In this musical ode, forever bold.

Musical composition

Enchanting orchestral arrangement with sweeping strings and delicate harp, capturing the magic of love.

Cmaj7 - Gm7 - Am7 - Fmaj7 (Repeat).

These chords are played in sequence and repeated throughout the arrangement.

Note: The myth of Eros and Psyche unfolds like a tapestry woven with threads of mortal beauty and divine desire. In these lyrical verses, choral rendition, and epic retelling, we explore the intricacies of their love, a tale that transcends the boundaries between gods and mortals.

Narrative retelling

In the realm of ancient Greece, amidst the towering columns of marble and the whispers of the olive groves, there lived a mortal princess named Psyche. She was blessed with unparalleled beauty, so radiant that it stirred the envy of the gods themselves. But despite her divine allure, Psyche's heart yearned for something more, a love that transcended mortal bounds.

Meanwhile, on Mount Olympus, the realm of the gods, dwelled Eros, the mischievous god of love. Armed with his golden arrows, he delighted in weaving the threads of desire among mortals, yet his own heart remained untouched by love's enchantment.

One fateful day, the goddess Aphrodite, Eros' mother, grew jealous of Psyche's beauty and commanded her son to strike her with an arrow, causing her to fall in love with the vilest of creatures. But when Eros laid eyes upon Psyche, his heart was pierced by a different kind of arrow, one of genuine affection.

Unable to carry out his mother's bidding, Eros watched over Psyche from afar, drawn to her purity and grace. Moved by an irresistible impulse, he descended from Olympus and whisked Psyche away to a hidden palace, where he concealed his true identity and visited her only under the cover of darkness.

In the soft glow of candlelight, Eros, and Psyche's bond blossomed, their hearts entwined in a love that defied all odds. But as whispers of Psyche's mysterious lover spread throughout the land, envy once again reared its ugly head.

Psyche's jealous sisters, consumed by bitterness and resentment, conspired to uncover the identity of her secret admirer. Feigning concern, they convinced Psyche that her lover must be a monstrous serpent lurking in the shadows, urging her to take a lamp and dagger to rid herself of the vile creature.

In the stillness of the night, Psyche crept to her lover's side, trembling with fear and uncertainty. But as she raised the lamp, its light revealed not a serpent but the breathtaking visage of Eros, the god of love himself.

Filled with remorse for doubting her beloved, Psyche's heart overflowed with love and gratitude. With trembling hands, she extinguished the lamp and embraced Eros, pledging her eternal devotion to him.

Touched by Psyche's unwavering faith and loyalty, Eros revealed his true identity and confessed his love for her. And in that moment, their union was blessed by the gods, their love immortalized for eternity.

From that day forth, Eros and Psyche reigned as king and queen of the heart, their love serving as a beacon of hope and inspiration for all who dared to believe in the transformative power of true love. And as the ages passed and empires rose and fell, their story endured, a timeless testament to the enduring strength of love's embrace.

Choral rendition

In ancient Greece's realm, where marble columns stand,
And whispers echo through the olive groves grand,
Lived Psyche, a princess with beauty divine,
Envy of gods, her radiance did shine.

Eros, on Olympus, god of love so sly,
With golden arrows, he wove desire's tie,
But his own heart untouched by love's sweet spell,
Till he met Psyche, then all was not well.

Aphrodite, his mother, grew jealous and sly,
Commanded her son, make Psyche's heart sigh,
But Eros, struck differently, with love so true,
Watched over Psyche, his affection grew.

He whisked her away to a palace concealed,
In darkness, their love tenderly revealed,
Yet envy crept in, sisters filled with disdain,
And Psyche's love was put to a cruel strain.

They whispered of serpents and monsters in fright,
Till Psyche believed, in the dead of the night,
With lamp and dagger, she sought out the beast,

But found her true love, her fears released.

Eros, revealed, confessed his love so pure,
Their union blessed, their devotion sure,
As king and queen of hearts, their love did bloom,
A timeless tale of love's eternal room.

Reflections and insights

In the retelling of Eros and Psyche's timeless tale, we glimpse the complexities of love, its power to ignite the soul, its ability to transcend boundaries, and its capacity to endure even the darkest of trials. Through the characters of Psyche and Eros, we explore the depths of human emotion, fear, doubt, jealousy, but also unwavering devotion, trust, and redemption.

At its core, this story speaks to the universal longing for connection and understanding, reminding us that love is not always straightforward, but it is always worth fighting for. In Psyche's journey from doubt to faith, from darkness to light, we find echoes of our own struggles and triumphs, a reflection of the human experience writ large.

And in Eros' unwavering love and sacrifice, we discover the transformative power of love to heal and redeem, to transcend even the boundaries between mortal and immortal. Through their union, we are reminded that love knows no bounds, that it is the greatest force in the universe, capable of conquering even the most formidable of obstacles.

Chapter 2: Melodies of Eternal Longing

Orpheus and Eurydice: A Lyrical Ode

Prologue

This beautiful ode is a retelling of the myth of Orpheus and Eurydice from Greek mythology.

In the echoes of eternal night,
Where shadows dance in pale moonlight,
An ode unfolds with mournful grace,
Of Orpheus and Eurydice's haunting embrace.

With lyre in hand and heart so bold,
Orpheus sings to the underworld's cold.
Eurydice, his love, in shadows lain,

A soul's lament in sorrow's refrain.

Through Stygian depths, Orpheus delves,
Where rivers flow, and darkness swells.
Eurydice's shade, a fleeting light,
In realms of shadow, veiled from sight.

In the abyss where silence reigns,
Orpheus' melodies soothe love's pains.
Eurydice's name, a whispered plea,
In love's embrace, they both decree.

A minstrel's plea, a lover's vow,
Orpheus' lyre resounds somehow.
Yet fate's decree, a tragic wail,
In love's embrace, forever they sail.

So in the halls of Hades' keep,
Their love's eternal vigil to reap.
An ode sung of love's enduring hue,
Of Orpheus and Eurydice, in shadows true.

Musical composition

Soulful and melancholic musical ode with haunting vocals and acoustic instrumentation, reflecting the depths of longing.

Em - Cmaj7 - G - D/F# (Repeat)

These chords are played in sequence and repeated throughout the arrangement.

Note: The myth of Orpheus and Eurydice sings of a love so deep that it transcends the boundaries between life and death. In these lyrical verses, choral rendition, and epic retelling, we delve into the poignant melodies that echo through the underworld and beyond.

Narrative retelling

In the ancient land of Thrace, where the rivers whisper secrets and the forests echo with the songs of nymphs, there lived a gifted musician named Orpheus. His melodies were so enchanting that they could soothe the fiercest of beasts and bring tears to the eyes of gods.

But despite his divine talent, Orpheus harbored a deep sorrow within his heart. For he had once been blessed with the love of a beautiful maiden named Eurydice. Their love was pure and true, their souls intertwined in a bond that seemed destined to last for eternity.

Yet, on their wedding day, tragedy struck. As Eurydice wandered through the sun-dappled glades, she was bitten by a venomous serpent and fell into a deep slumber from which she could not awaken. Orpheus, consumed by grief, vowed to journey to the depths of the underworld to reclaim his beloved.

With his lyre in hand and a song upon his lips, Orpheus descended into the realm of Hades, where the spirits of the dead roamed in eternal darkness. Through the shadowed caverns and across the river Styx, he sang of love and loss, his music piercing the veil between the worlds of the living and the dead.

Moved by the haunting strains of Orpheus' song, even the sternest of souls wept tears of sorrow. And when he reached the throne of Hades and Persephone, the lord and lady of the underworld, they too were moved by his plight.

Touched by Orpheus' devotion, Hades agreed to grant him his request. But there was one condition: Orpheus must lead Eurydice out of the underworld without once looking back until they had reached the world of the living.

With a heart filled with hope, Orpheus embraced his beloved and began the journey back to the surface. As they ascended through the dimly lit passages, the echo of Orpheus' song reverberated through the caverns, guiding them toward the light.

But as they neared the threshold of the underworld, doubt began to gnaw at Orpheus' heart. Fearing that Eurydice might not be following behind him, he turned to look upon her face, despite the warnings of Hades.

In that moment, tragedy struck once again. For as Orpheus met Eurydice's gaze, she began to fade away before his very eyes, pulled back into the depths of the underworld by the cruel hands of fate.

With a cry of anguish, Orpheus reached out to grasp his beloved, but she slipped through his fingers like mist, leaving only the echo of her voice lingering in the air. And as the last notes of Orpheus' song faded into silence, he was left alone once more, his heart shattered by the bitter sting of loss.

From that day forth, Orpheus wandered the earth in mourning, his songs now filled with sorrow and longing. But even in his darkest hours, the memory of Eurydice remained etched upon his soul, a beacon of light in the endless night.

And though their love had been torn asunder by the cruel whims of fate, Orpheus vowed to carry Eurydice's memory with him always, a testament to the enduring power of love to transcend even death itself.

Choral rendition

In Thrace's ancient land where whispers abound,
Orpheus, a musician, with melodies profound,
His lyre's enchantment could calm the wildest beast,
But sorrow within him, his heart did feast.

Eurydice, his love, so pure and bright,
Their souls entwined, a radiant light,
But tragedy struck on their wedding day,
A serpent's bite stole her away.

To the underworld, Orpheus dared to descend,
With love's song, his journey he'd amend,
Through darkness and shadow, his music led the way,
To reclaim his love, come what may.

Hades and Persephone, moved by his plea,
Agreed to release her, but with a decree,
No looking back till the world of light,
Or lose her forever, out of sight.

With hope in his heart, they journeyed on,
But doubt crept in as they approached the dawn,
He turned to see, against the pact,

And Eurydice slipped, destiny's act.

With anguish in his soul, Orpheus cried,
His love, like mist, away did glide,
Yet her memory lingered, a guiding flame,
In his songs, he whispered her name.

Though fate tore them apart, love's bond remained,
In Orpheus' heart, forever ingrained,
A testament to love's enduring might,
Even in death, its radiant light.

Reflections and insights

In the retelling of the tragic tale of Orpheus and Eurydice, we are reminded of the fragile nature of love and the relentless grip of fate. Through the characters of Orpheus and Eurydice, we witness the depths of human emotion, the joy of love found, the agony of love lost, and the unyielding determination to defy the odds in the pursuit of true happiness.

At its heart, this story serves as a poignant reminder of the power of love to transcend even the darkest of depths. Orpheus' journey into the underworld symbolizes the lengths to which one will go for love, even if it means facing the greatest of challenges and braving the most treacherous of paths.

But amidst the tragedy and heartache lies a glimmer of hope, a testament to the enduring strength of the human spirit. For even in the face of overwhelming odds, Orpheus' love for Eurydice remains unwavering, a beacon of light in the darkness of despair. And though their story may end in sorrow, their love lives on as a timeless testament to the beauty and resilience of the human heart.

Chapter 3: A Symphony of Transformation

Apollo and Daphne: A Lyrical Ode

Prologue

This beautiful ode is a retelling of the myth of Apollo and Daphne from Greek mythology.

In the realm where nature's melodies soar,
Began Apollo and Daphne's lore.
A tale of love in lyrical sway,
Where gods and nymphs dance in play.

Apollo, radiant in the sun's embrace,
Daphne, in shadow's gentle grace.
In love's pursuit, Apollo's fervent flame,

Nature's symphony sings their name.

Daphne, amidst the forest's verdant veil,
Apollo's love, a destined tale.
Bark and leaf, her form entwined,
Love's metamorphosis, forever enshrined.

In the murmuring leaves, Apollo weeps,
As Daphne to laurel form leaps.
Their love, in nature's timeless design,
A symphony of souls intertwined.

Musical composition

Majestic orchestral symphony with dynamic shifts, mirroring the transformative journey of love.

Dmaj - Gmaj - Em - A (Repeat)

These chords are played in sequence and repeated throughout the arrangement.

Note: The myth of Apollo and Daphne unfolds as a symphony of transformation, where love takes root in the eternal dance of nature. In these lyrical verses, choral rendition, and epic retelling, we explore the metamorphosis of a nymph escaping the god of the sun.

Narrative retelling

In the golden light of ancient Greece, where the laurel trees whispered secrets to the wind and the sun god Apollo ruled the heavens, there lived a maiden named Daphne. She was as graceful as the swaying branches and as radiant as the dawn, her beauty captivating all who beheld her.

But despite her many admirers, Daphne had no interest in love or romance. She preferred the company of the forest nymphs and the music of the birdsong to the advances of mortal men and gods alike.

Among those who pursued Daphne was Apollo, the god of prophecy and music, whose heart was captivated by her ethereal beauty. Determined to win her affection, Apollo showered Daphne with gifts and serenaded her with songs of love, but she remained unmoved by his charms.

Frustrated by Daphne's indifference, Apollo resolved to make her his own, regardless of her feelings. With a heart consumed by desire, he pursued her through the forest, his footsteps echoing through the ancient groves as he closed in on his quarry.

But as Apollo reached out to grasp Daphne's hand, she recoiled in fear, her heart pounding with terror at the thought of being claimed by the sun god. With a desperate cry, she called upon her father, the river god Peneus, to save her from Apollo's advances.

Moved by his daughter's plea, Peneus transformed Daphne into a laurel tree, her slender limbs stretching skyward as her feet took root in the earth below. In an instant, she was transformed, her flesh turning to bark and her hair to leaves, her beauty frozen in time for all eternity.

Heartbroken by Daphne's transformation, Apollo stood frozen in shock, his outstretched arms reaching for the tree that had once been his beloved. But try as he might, he could not reverse the spell that had been cast, and he was left to mourn the loss of his love for all time.

And so, to this day, the laurel tree remains a symbol of Apollo's unrequited love, its leaves forever green and its branches forever reaching toward the sun. And though Daphne may never return Apollo's affections, her beauty endures in the whispering winds and the rustling leaves, a reminder of the power of love and the price of desire.

Choral rendition

In ancient Greece's golden light,
Where laurel trees whispered, oh so bright,
Daphne dwelled, a maiden fair,
Her beauty beyond compare.

But love's allure, she did defy,
Preferring forest's nymphs' soft sigh,
Apollo, god of prophecy bold,
His heart for Daphne, did enfold.

With gifts and songs, he wooed in vain,
Her heart unmoved, amidst the plain,
Through ancient groves, he chased her down,
His love for her, a golden crown.

But as he reached for her gentle hand,
She fled from him, to forest's stand,
A cry for help, to her father dear,
To save her from Apollo's fear.

Peneus heard his daughter's plea,
Transformed her into a laurel tree,
Her beauty frozen, for all to see,

A symbol of love's tragedy.

Apollo stood, his heart in pain,
His beloved, lost, but not in vain,
For in the laurel, she'll always be,
A reminder of love's mystery.

Though Apollo's love may never wane,
Daphne's form, forever changed,
In whispering winds and rustling leaves,
Her spirit in nature, eternally grieves.

Reflections and insights

In the retelling of the tragic tale of Apollo and Daphne, we are confronted with the timeless themes of desire, pursuit, and the consequences of unchecked passion. Through the characters of Apollo and Daphne, we witness the clash between divine will and mortal agency, as well as the transformative power of nature to resist the advances of the divine.

At its core, this story serves as a cautionary tale of the dangers of obsession and the importance of respecting the boundaries of others. Apollo's relentless pursuit of Daphne, driven by his own desires and ambitions, ultimately leads to her transformation and his own heartbreak.

But amidst the tragedy lies a deeper truth, a reminder of the resilience of the human spirit and the enduring power of nature to assert itself against even the mightiest of gods. Daphne's transformation into a laurel tree symbolizes her liberation from Apollo's grasp and her embrace of her own identity and autonomy.

As we reflect on the story of Apollo and Daphne, may we be reminded of the importance of empathy, consent, and mutual respect in all our relationships.

Chapter 4: Tragedy in Mulberry Red

Pyramus and Thisbe: A Lyrical Ode

Prologue

This beautiful ode is a retelling of the myth of Pyramus and Thisbe from Greek mythology.

In the shadows of evening's embrace,
A lyrical ode unfolds a tragic race.
Of Pyramus and Thisbe's love so true,
Their tale, in hues of mulberry, imbued.

In deepened shadows, clandestine meet,
Their passion veiled, secrets discreet.
Yet a wall, stark witness, did stand,

An obstacle to love's tender hand.

In hues of mulberry, destiny sealed,
In sorrow's garden, emotions revealed.
Thisbe's veil, by cruel fate's kiss,
Pyramus' lament, in mournful abyss.

In shadowed depths, their love does wane,
In mulberry tones, hearts bear the strain.
Two souls entwined in death's gentle grace,
A lyrical ode sings of love's tragic embrace.

Musical composition

Dramatic opera with intense vocal duets and a sorrowful orchestral backdrop, evoking the tragic essence.

Am – G – F – E (Repeat)

These chords are played in sequence and repeated throughout the arrangement.

Note: The tale of Pyramus and Thisbe unfolds as a tragedy painted in mulberry red, where love's bloom withers in the shadowed garden. In these lyrical verses, choral rendition, and epic retelling, we explore the tragic fate of two lovers separated by a wall.

Narrative retelling

In the ancient city of Babylon, where the walls were adorned with intricate mosaics and the streets hummed with the chatter of merchants, there lived two young lovers named Pyramus and Thisbe. Their love was as deep as the Euphrates River and as enduring as the desert sands, their hearts bound together by an unbreakable bond.

Yet, despite their love, Pyramus and Thisbe were forbidden from being together, for their families were bitter rivals, locked in a feud that spanned generations. Undeterred by the enmity that divided them, the two lovers would steal moments together in secret, their meetings hidden beneath the shadow of an ancient mulberry tree that grew at the edge of the city.

But one fateful day, tragedy struck. As Pyramus and Thisbe planned to meet beneath the mulberry tree, a ferocious lion emerged from the nearby forest, its mane ablaze with fury. Terrified, Thisbe fled, leaving behind her veil as a token of her presence.

When Pyramus arrived at their meeting place and discovered Thisbe's abandoned veil, he was overcome with grief and despair. Believing that his beloved had been slain by the lion, he resolved to take his own life rather than live without her.

Drawing his sword, Pyramus plunged it into his chest, his blood staining the earth beneath him as he uttered Thisbe's name one final time. And as his life ebbed away, the mulberry tree drank deeply of his blood, its once-white berries turning crimson in his memory.

Meanwhile, Thisbe, having narrowly escaped the lion's clutches, returned to find her beloved lying lifeless beneath the mulberry tree. Heartbroken and distraught, she took up Pyramus' sword and joined him in death, her final breath a whispered lament for the love they had lost.

And so, in death as in life, Pyramus and Thisbe remained united, their love immortalized in the crimson berries of the mulberry tree and the whispered echoes of their tragic tale. And though their families continued to feud, their love served as a testament to the enduring power of passion and devotion, a beacon of hope in a world torn apart by strife.

Choral rendition

In Babylon, where mosaics gleam,
Pyramus and Thisbe's love did teem,
Forbidden by their families' feud,
Yet bound by love, their hearts pursued.

Beneath the mulberry tree's shade,
In secret, their love they displayed,
But tragedy struck, a lion's roar,
Their love, now shaken to its core.

Thisbe fled, her veil left behind,
Pyramus, in anguish, he did find,
Believing his love to be no more,
He chose to join her on death's shore.

With sword in hand, he took his life,
Amidst the pain, amidst the strife,
The mulberry tree, its berries red,
In memory of the lovers dead.

Thisbe returned, to find him there,
Her heart, consumed by love's despair,
With Pyramus, she chose to die,

Their love, forever in the sky.

In life and death, they were as one,
Their tale of love, forever spun,
A testament to passion's might,
In Babylon's eternal light.

Reflections and insights

In the retelling of the tragic tale of Pyramus and Thisbe, we are confronted with the timeless themes of forbidden love, tragedy, and the power of fate. Through the characters of Pyramus and Thisbe, we witness the profound depths of human emotion, the joy of love found, the agony of love lost, and the ultimate sacrifice made in the name of devotion.

At its heart, this story serves as a poignant reminder of the consequences of division and discord, as well as the enduring strength of love to transcend even the greatest of obstacles. Pyramus and Thisbe's love, though thwarted by the enmity of their families and the cruel hand of fate, endures beyond death itself, a testament to the unbreakable bond that binds two souls together.

But amidst the tragedy lies a glimmer of hope, a reminder of the resilience of the human spirit and the enduring power of love to conquer even the darkest of circumstances. Pyramus and Thisbe's love, though cut short by tragedy, serves as a beacon of light in a world consumed by strife, inspiring us to cherish each moment with those we hold dear and to never lose faith in the transformative power of love.

Chapter 5: Envy's Dark Whispers

Cupid and Psyche's Sisters: A Lyrical Ode

Prologue

This beautiful ode is a retelling of the myth of Cupid (Eros) and Psyche's Sisters from Greek mythology.

In the garden where envy weaves its intricate threads,
Cupid's arrows, like autumn leaves, softly tread.
Psyche's beauty, a radiant beam in love's pure light,
In envy's shadow, a fleeting dream takes flight.

Sisters' whispers, like a chilling breeze, echo with strife,
In envy's grasp, they stumble in the dance of life.

Yet love prevails, in Eros' tender sight,
An ode sung of love's unyielding flight.

Through trials dark, their love does fiercely soar,
In envy's grip, they crave, yearn for more.
But Cupid's arrows, a force divine, entwine,
In love's embrace, they eternally shine.

So let this ode forever proclaim and swell,
Of love's triumph over envy's knell.
In the garden where true love finds its guise,
Cupid and Psyche dance under starlit skies.

Musical composition

Mysterious and suspenseful soundtrack with ethereal voices and electronic elements, portraying the dark whispers of envy.

Bm - E - A - F#m (Repeat)

These chords are played in sequence and repeated throughout the arrangement.

Note: The story of Cupid and Psyche's Sisters reveals the dark whispers of envy that threaten to overshadow the brilliance of love. In these lyrical verses, choral rendition, and epic retelling, we explore the jealousy that seeks to cast a shadow on Psyche's divine connection.

Narrative retelling

Once upon a time, in a world where love reigned supreme and envy lurked in the shadows, there lived three sisters: Psyche, the fairest of them all, and her two jealous siblings. While Psyche's beauty shone like the brightest star in the heavens, her sisters harbored bitterness in their hearts, consumed by envy at her radiant glow.

As Psyche basked in the adoration of suitors from far and wide, her sisters seethed with jealousy, their hearts twisted with resentment at her good fortune. Unable to bear the sight of their sister's happiness, they conspired to sabotage her newfound joy.

One fateful day, as Psyche reveled in the company of her beloved, the god of love himself, Cupid, her sisters sought to sow seeds of doubt and mistrust in her heart. Feigning concern, they whispered lies of betrayal and deceit, casting doubt upon Cupid's intentions and questioning the sincerity of his love.

But despite their efforts to poison Psyche's mind, she remained steadfast in her devotion to Cupid, her heart unwavering in its trust. Undeterred by her sisters' malicious words, she chose to believe in the power of love and the purity of her beloved's intentions.

Moved by Psyche's unwavering faith, Cupid resolved to put her sisters' envy to the test. With a flick of his golden arrows, he revealed their true nature, exposing the darkness that lurked within their hearts and the depth of their jealousy.

In the end, it was not Psyche's beauty or Cupid's love that triumphed, but the power of trust and faith to overcome the poison of envy. And though Psyche's sisters may have been consumed by bitterness, she emerged from the ordeal stronger and wiser than before, her love for Cupid shining brighter than ever.

And so, in a world where envy seeks to tear love apart, Psyche and Cupid's love serves as a beacon of hope, a reminder that true love knows no bounds and that trust and faith are the strongest weapons against the darkness that seeks to divide us.

Choral rendition

Once upon a time, in love's domain,
Three sisters dwelled, each with disdain,
Psyche, fairest of them all,
Her beauty bright, her sisters' fall.

Envy lurked in shadows deep,
As Psyche's love began to creep,
Cupid's arrow struck her heart,
Her sisters' envy tore apart.

Whispers of betrayal, deceit abound,
But Psyche's faith, forever sound,
In love's embrace, she chose to stay,
Her trust in Cupid, come what may.

Moved by her unwavering trust,
Cupid revealed their envy's crust,
In the end, it was trust that won,
Over envy's darkness, love's bright sun.

Though bitterness consumed her kin,
Psyche emerged, her heart within,
Stronger, wiser, her love declared,

In Cupid's arms, no longer scared.

In a world where envy seeks to maim,
Their love, a beacon, forever flame,
For trust and faith, against the night,
Shine brighter than envy's blight.

Reflections and insights

In the retelling of the story of Cupid and Psyche's sisters, we delve into the complexities of human emotion, love, envy, trust, and betrayal. Through the characters of Psyche and her sisters, we witness the destructive power of envy and the transformative nature of trust and faith.

At its core, this story serves as a cautionary tale of the dangers of succumbing to jealousy and resentment. Psyche's sisters, consumed by envy, sought to undermine her happiness, and destroy her trust in the love she had found. Yet, in the face of their malicious intentions, Psyche remained steadfast in her belief in the power of love and the sincerity of Cupid's affections.

Through her unwavering faith, Psyche not only triumphed over her sisters' envy but also emerged stronger and more resilient than before. Her love for Cupid, fueled by trust and faith, proved to be an unbreakable bond, capable of overcoming even the darkest of challenges. And may we find solace in the knowledge that, even in the face of adversity, love has the power to conquer all.

Chapter 6: A Pomegranate's Pact

Hades and Persephone: A Lyrical Ode

Prologue

This beautiful ode is a retelling of the myth of Hades and Persephone from Greek mythology.

In the realm where shadows hold sway,
An ode sings of love's bittersweet play.
Of Hades and Persephone's rare embrace,
In depths of darkness, their bond finds grace.

Hades, sovereign of the underworld's reign,
Persephone's bloom in eternal chain.
Sealed by seeds of pomegranate's lore,

Their love transcends, forevermore.

Through Stygian depths, their passion unfurls,
In darkest night, their hearts entwirl.
Persephone, torn 'twixt light and shade,
In Hades' realm, her choice is made.

In shadows' embrace, where secrets reside,
Persephone's bloom, her beauty defied.
A hymn to love in darkness sung,
In Hades' kingdom, their souls are one.

Musical composition

Dark, ambient, and orchestral fusion capturing the underworld's mystique, with haunting vocals and rich instrumentation.

Dm - Bb - C - Am (Repeat)

These chords are played in sequence and repeated throughout the arrangement.

Note: The myth of Hades and Persephone unfolds as an ode to love's duality, where the underworld's shadows dance with the bloom of eternal spring. In these lyrical verses, choral rendition, and epic retelling, we explore the union of the god of the underworld and the goddess of spring.

Narrative retelling

In the realm of the underworld, where shadows danced upon the river Styx, and the souls of the departed whispered secrets to the night, there ruled a god of darkness and death named Hades. His kingdom was a place of eternal gloom, where the spirits of the dead wandered aimlessly through the darkened halls of his palace.

Yet, amidst the shadows, there dwelled a goddess of spring and renewal named Persephone. Daughter of the earth goddess Demeter, Persephone's beauty shone like a beacon of light in the darkness of the underworld, her laughter like the tinkling of bells in the stillness of the night.

One fateful day, as Persephone roamed the fields of the mortal realm, gathering flowers in her basket, she caught the eye of Hades, the lord of the underworld. Enthralled by her beauty, he resolved to make her his queen, to rule by his side for all eternity.

With a mighty roar, Hades emerged from the depths of the earth, his chariot drawn by four black horses as he swept Persephone away to his kingdom below. And though she struggled against his grasp, her fate was sealed, her destiny entwined with his in an eternal dance of darkness and light.

As the seasons passed, Persephone found herself torn between the darkness of the underworld and the warmth of the mortal realm above. Though she longed for the sunlit fields and the embrace of her mother, she found solace in the love of Hades, whose heart had been softened by her presence.

But as the months turned to years, Persephone's absence from the mortal realm brought despair to the earth, causing crops to wither and flowers to fade. In her grief, Demeter beseeched Zeus, king of the gods, to intervene and bring her daughter back to the world above.

Moved by Demeter's pleas, Zeus decreed that Persephone would spend half of the year with Hades in the underworld and the other half with her mother in the mortal realm. And so, it was that Persephone became the goddess of the seasons, her presence heralding the arrival of spring and the renewal of life.

And though her love for Hades endured, Persephone's heart remained forever divided between the darkness of the underworld and the light of the mortal realm, her destiny forever entwined with the cycle of life and death, renewal, and rebirth.

Choral rendition

In the realm of shadows, dark and deep,
Where souls of the departed sleep,
Hades ruled with an iron hand,
In the underworld's eternal land.

But amidst the gloom, a light did shine,
Persephone, with beauty divine,
Daughter of Demeter, goddess of spring,
Her laughter, like bells, did softly ring.

Caught in Hades' gaze, she was swept away,
To rule by his side, night and day,
Though torn between darkness and light,
Her fate entwined, in eternal flight.

As seasons turned, her heart did sway,
Between the realms, night and day,
Though she longed for the mortal land,
Love softened Hades' dark command.

But Demeter's grief, the earth did cry,
Crops withered, flowers did die,
Zeus decreed, a compromise,

Half with Hades, half in the skies.

Persephone, goddess of the seasons, became,
Bringing renewal, life's eternal flame,
Her heart forever divided, yet love did endure,
In the cycle of life, forever pure.

Reflections and insights

In the retelling of the myth of Hades and Persephone, we are drawn into the timeless dance between darkness and light, death and rebirth. Through the characters of Hades and Persephone, we explore the intricacies of love, sacrifice, and the cyclical nature of existence.

At its heart, this story serves as a reminder of the delicate balance that exists within the natural world and the interconnectedness of all things. Persephone's journey between the underworld and the mortal realm mirrors the changing of the seasons, a constant cycle of death and renewal that shapes the world around us.

But amidst the darkness, there is also light, and amidst death, there is also rebirth. Persephone's love for Hades, though born from darkness, brings light to the underworld and warmth to the hearts of its inhabitants. And though she must spend half of the year in the shadows, her presence heralds the arrival of spring and the promise of new life.

Chapter 7: Golden Fleece of Betrayal

Jason and Medea: A Lyrical Ode

Prologue

This beautiful ode is a retelling of the myth of Jason and Medea from Greek mythology.

In the realm where legends roam free,
An ode unfolds of hearts turned to stone, you see.
Of Jason and Medea, a tale both fierce and bold,
Their saga ensnared in betrayal's hold.

Jason, seeker of glory's acclaim,
Medea, with power, and a name aflame.
For a fleece of gold, the hero strives,
Yet love's true worth, a sacrifice thrives.

In potions brewed, by magic's design,
Medea's love, a venomous line.
Betrayal's sting, a bitter end unfurls,
A sorceress scorned, and a hero in whirls.

In Colchis' realm, where shadows waltz tall,
Jason and Medea, ensnared in a thrall.
A kingdom charred, in the flames it meets,
A ballad of love, with treacherous beats.

So let this ode echo through time's reign,
Of betrayal's toll, and the hurt it sustains.
In the weave of love's tapestry, where destinies align,
Jason and Medea, their legacy shall shine.

Musical composition

Epic film score with powerful choirs and intense orchestration, conveying the grandeur of betrayal.

F#m - C#m - E - B (Repeat).

These chords are played in sequence and repeated throughout the arrangement.

Note: The tale of Jason and Medea weaves a complex narrative of love, betrayal, and the consequences of heartbreak. In these lyrical verses, choral rendition, and epic retelling, we delve into the tragic saga of a hero and a sorceress whose love becomes entangled in the threads of destiny.

Narrative retelling

In the ancient land of Greece, where heroes walked among mortals and gods toyed with the lives of men, there lived a hero named Jason. Fated by prophecy to reclaim he Golden Fleece, Jason embarked on a perilous journey with a band of fearless adventurers known as the Argonauts.

But it was not the quest for the Golden Fleece that would define Jason's fate, but rather the love he found along the way. For it was during his quest that he encountered the sorceress Medea, daughter of the king of Colchis and guardian of the Golden Fleece.

Enchanted by her beauty and captivated by her magic, Jason found himself drawn to Medea in a way he had never known before. And though their love was forbidden by fate and opposed by their enemies, they were bound together by a bond that transcended the boundaries of mortal understanding.

With Medea's help, Jason succeeded in obtaining the Golden Fleece, but their triumph was short-lived. Faced with betrayal and treachery, they were forced to flee Colchis, pursued by the wrath of King Aeëtes and his vengeful allies.

In their flight, Jason and Medea faced countless trials and tribulations, their love tested at every turn. But through it all, they remained steadfast in their devotion to one another, united in their quest for freedom and redemption.

Yet, as they neared the shores of their homeland, tragedy struck. In a fit of jealousy and rage, Jason betrayed Medea, casting her aside in favor of a political marriage that would secure his place as king.

Devastated by Jason's betrayal, Medea's love turned to bitterness and vengeance. With a heart filled with rage and a mind consumed by madness, she unleashed the full extent of her sorcery upon her enemies, wreaking havoc and devastation in her wake.

In the end, Jason paid the ultimate price for his betrayal, his kingdom destroyed, and his children slain by Medea's hand. And though Medea's vengeance brought her no solace, she remained forever haunted by the memory of the love she had lost and the darkness that had consumed her soul.

And so, in the annals of history, the tale of Jason and Medea endures as a cautionary tale of love, betrayal, and the consequences of forsaking the bonds that bind us together. And though their love may have been doomed from the start, its legacy lives on as a testament to the power of passion and the dangers of unchecked ambition.

Choral rendition

In ancient Greece, where heroes roamed,
Jason sought the Golden Fleece, his home,
With the Argonauts, a fearless band,
He ventured forth, across the land.

But 'twas not gold that filled his heart,
But love he found, a sorceress' art,
Medea, fair with magic's touch,
Their love forbidden, yet meant so much.

With her aid, the fleece was won,
But betrayal followed, their journey done,
Forced to flee, pursued by hate,
Their love tested, by cruel fate.

Through trials and tribulations, they strove,
Bound by love, their hearts wove,
Yet tragedy struck, on their return,
As jealousy and rage did burn.

Jason's betrayal, Medea's wrath,
A kingdom lost, in aftermath,
Children slain, by sorcery's might,

Love turned to darkness, in the night.

Their tale, a caution, of love betrayed,
And consequences, forever paid,
In history's annals, their legacy told,
Of passion's power, and ambition's hold.

Reflections and insights

In the retelling of the tragic tale of Jason and Medea, we are confronted with the complexities of love, betrayal, and the consequences of our actions. Through the characters of Jason and Medea, we delve into the depths of human emotion, the ecstasy of love found, the agony of love lost, and the destructive power of jealousy and vengeance.

At its core, this story serves as a cautionary tale of the dangers of forsaking love in pursuit of ambition and power. Jason's betrayal of Medea, driven by his desire for political gain, ultimately leads to his downfall, as well as the destruction of all he holds dear.

But amidst the tragedy, there is also a deeper truth, a reminder of the resilience of the human spirit and the capacity for redemption and forgiveness. Though Medea's actions are born from a place of pain and betrayal, her love for Jason remains unwavering, even in the face of his betrayal. And may we find solace in the knowledge that, even in the darkest of times, there is always hope for redemption and forgiveness, if only we have the courage to seek it.

Chapter 8: Beauty's Price

Helen and Paris: A Lyrical Ode

Prologue

This beautiful ode is a retelling of the myth of Helen and Paris from Greek mythology.

In the realm where legends reside,
A tale of love and war, we confide.
Of Helen and Paris, an ancient lore,
Where beauty's allure opens a timeless door.

Helen, regal with beauty's grace,
Paris, princely, love's embrace.
A stolen kiss, a destiny bound,
A saga of love, profound and profound.

Across the seas, a fleet did glide,

To Troy's shores, fate did decide.
Helen's allure, a tale untold,
In love's embrace, their hearts enfold.

Within Troy's walls, passions entwine,
Helen and Paris, in love divine.
A kingdom's fall, flames do ignite,
A story of love, in sorrow's night.

So let this ode of melody ring,
Of beauty's price, and the pain it brings.
In history's scroll, their love engraved,
Helen and Paris, their destiny saved.

Musical composition

Romantic orchestral waltz with lush strings and woodwinds, encapsulating the allure of Helen's beauty.

D - G - Em - A (Repeat).

These chords are played in sequence and repeated throughout the arrangement.

Note: The myth of Helen and Paris unveils the beauty that launched a thousand ships and the consequences of love's irresistible allure. In these lyrical verses, choral rendition, and epic retelling, we explore the tale of a queen and a prince whose passion sparks a war.

Narrative retelling

In the sun-drenched city of Troy, where the walls gleamed like burnished gold, and the laughter of its people echoed through the streets, there lived a prince named Paris. Handsome and charming, Paris was the favored son of King Priam and Queen Hecuba, beloved by all who knew him.

But Paris was not content with the life of a prince. Restless and eager for adventure, he yearned to make his mark upon the world and carve out his own destiny. And so, when the opportunity presented itself, Paris set sail for the distant shores of Sparta, where fate would intervene in the most unexpected of ways.

For it was in Sparta that Paris encountered the most beautiful woman he had ever seen, Helen, the queen of Sparta, whose beauty was said to rival that of the goddesses themselves. Enchanted by her radiance, Paris found himself irresistibly drawn to her, his heart consumed by a love so fierce and undeniable that it defied all reason.

But Helen was no ordinary woman. She was the wife of King Menelaus, ruler of Sparta, and her beauty had sparked the flames of desire in the hearts of men across the land. And though she felt a stirring of emotion for Paris, she was bound by duty and honor to her husband, unable to act upon the forbidden desires that raged within her.

Undeterred by the obstacles that stood in their way, Paris and Helen embarked upon a passionate affair, their love blossoming in the shadows of secrecy and deceit. But their happiness was short-lived, for news of their betrayal soon reached the ears of King Menelaus, who vowed vengeance upon those who had wronged him.

And so, the stage was set for a conflict that would shake the foundations of the ancient world, a war that would come to be known as the Trojan War, a conflict that would ultimately lead to the downfall of a great city and the loss of countless lives.

But amidst the chaos and destruction, Paris and Helen remained steadfast in their love, their hearts forever entwined in a bond that transcended the boundaries of time and space. And though their actions would bring about the downfall of Troy, their love would endure as a testament to the power of passion and the enduring legacy of forbidden desire.

Choral rendition

In Troy's sun-kissed land, where laughter did ring,
Lived Prince Paris, a favored king,
Restless and eager, he sought his fate,
In Sparta's arms, he'd soon elate.

For there he found, the fairest sight,
Helen, whose beauty shone so bright,
Irresistible, his love did grow,
A passion fierce, that none could know.

But Helen, bound by duty's chain,
Her heart conflicted, her love in vain,
Yet Paris' charm, it held her tight,
In shadows deep, their love took flight.

Their affair, a flame that burned,
In secrecy, their hearts yearned,
But Menelaus, betrayed and wroth,
Swore vengeance upon their troth.

And thus began the Trojan War,
A conflict fierce, a battle's roar,
But amidst the chaos, love did bloom,

In Paris' heart, in Helen's room.

Though Troy fell, in ashes lain,
Their love endured, amidst the pain,
A testament to passion's might,
In the darkness, shining bright.

Reflections and insights

In the retelling of the timeless tale of Helen and Paris, we are confronted with the complexities of love, duty, and the consequences of our actions. Through the characters of Helen and Paris, we delve into the depths of human emotion, the intoxicating allure of forbidden desire, the agony of betrayal, and the devastating impact of war.

At its core, this story serves as a cautionary tale of the destructive power of passion and the far-reaching consequences of selfish actions. Paris and Helen's reckless pursuit of love, driven by desire and passion, ultimately leads to the downfall of an entire city and the loss of countless lives.

But amidst the tragedy, there is also a deeper truth, a reminder of the resilience of the human spirit and the capacity for love to transcend even the darkest of times. Despite the chaos and destruction they leave in their wake, Paris and Helen's love endures as a testament to the enduring power of passion and the timeless allure of forbidden desire.

Chapter 9: A Golden Race of Love

Atalanta and Hippomenes: A Lyrical Ode

Prologue

This beautiful ode is a retelling of the myth of Atalanta and Hippomenes from Greek mythology.

In the realm where love holds its fiery chase,
   A lyrical ode of hearts in swift embrace.
Of Atalanta and Hippomenes, so bold,
   Their golden race, a tale retold.

Atalanta, fleet of foot and keen of eye,
Hippomenes, with cunning wiles sly.

In the race of gold, with apples cast,
Hippomenes' strategy held steadfast.

Atalanta, beguiled by the gleaming prize,
Hippomenes' cunning caught her eyes.
In golden apples, love's sweet decoy,
Atalanta's pace slowed in coy.

Through the race, a dance of fateful play,
Golden apples, love's intricate array.
Atalanta, ensnared by desire's fire,
Hippomenes' crafty heart conspire.

In the realm where love's enchantments sway,
Atalanta and Hippomenes' hearts find their way.
A union forged in a race so rare,
A hymn to love beyond compare.

Musical composition

Upbeat folk-pop with lively acoustic instruments, reflecting the excitement of the golden race.

G - D - Em - C (Repeat)

These chords are played in sequence and repeated throughout the arrangement.

Note: The myth of Atalanta and Hippomenes unfolds as a golden race where love is pursued with cunning and swiftness. In these lyrical verses, choral rendition, and epic retelling, we explore the love story of a hunter and a suitor whose golden apples lead to an enchanting union.

Narrative retelling

In the rugged hills of ancient Greece, where the forests teemed with wild beasts and the air was thick with the scent of pine, there lived a fearless huntress named Atalanta. Renowned for her beauty and unmatched skill with the bow, Atalanta roamed the wilderness with the grace of a deer and the swiftness of the wind.

But despite her prowess as a hunter, Atalanta harbored a secret longing, a desire to find a love that matched her own strength and spirit. And so, when she heard of a challenge issued by King Iasus, offering her hand in marriage to any man who could outrun her in a footrace, Atalanta saw her chance to find a suitor worthy of her affections.

Many brave suitors came from far and wide to test their mettle against Atalanta, but none could match her speed and agility. That is until Hippomenes, a handsome young man with a mischievous gleam in his eye, stepped forward to accept the challenge.

Undeterred by Atalanta's reputation as the fastest woman in Greece, Hippomenes devised a cunning plan to win her heart. As the race began, he dropped three golden apples, gifts from the goddess Aphrodite herself, in Atalanta's path, each one more tempting than the last.

Intrigued by the gleaming treasures lying before her, Atalanta paused to pick up the apples, her curiosity getting the better of her. And in that moment of hesitation,

Hippomenes surged ahead, his speed fueled by the power of love and desire.

Though Atalanta raced with all her might, she could not catch up to Hippomenes, who crossed the finish line victorious. And though she felt a pang of regret at her defeat, she also felt a stirring of something new, a spark of admiration for the man who had bested her in the race of love.

And so, Atalanta and Hippomenes were wed in a joyous ceremony, their love forged in the heat of competition and tempered by the trials they had faced together. And though their lives were filled with adventure and excitement, they remained forever bound by the golden thread of love that had brought them together.

In the end, it was not Atalanta's speed or strength that won her heart, but the courage and cunning of a man who dared to challenge her and the power of love to conquer even the mightiest of obstacles. And though their story may fade into legend with the passage of time, the love of Atalanta and Hippomenes would endure as a timeless testament to the enduring power of passion and perseverance.

Choral rendition

In ancient Greece's rugged land,
Atalanta roamed, a huntress grand,
With bow in hand and heart of fire,
She moved with grace, her spirit higher.

But beneath her strength, a longing burned,
For love that matched, her soul discerned,
When King Iasus issued his decree,
A race for love, to set her free.

Many came, to test their might,
But none could match her speed in flight,
Until Hippomenes, with a plan so bold,
To win her heart, he'd strive to hold.

With golden apples, gifts divine,
He tempted her, with each design,
And as she paused, to pick them near,
Hippomenes surged, without fear.

Though Atalanta raced with all her might,
Hippomenes won, in love's sweet flight,
Their union forged, in victory's glow,

In love's embrace, they'd forever grow.

With courage, cunning, they faced their fate,
In joyous union, they celebrate,
For love's power, it did prevail,
In Atalanta's heart, in Hippomenes' tale.

Though legends fade, with time's embrace,
Their love endures, in endless grace,
A testament to passion's flight,
In Atalanta's love, in Hippomenes' might.

Reflections and insights

In the retelling of the myth of Atalanta and Hippomenes, we are reminded of the transformative power of love and the unexpected ways in which it can shape our lives. Through the characters of Atalanta and Hippomenes, we explore the themes of courage, determination, and the pursuit of true love.

Atalanta, with her strength and independence, embodies the archetype of a strong and empowered woman. Her willingness to challenge societal norms and assert her agency in the pursuit of love sets her apart as a heroine of myth and legend.

Hippomenes, on the other hand, represents the power of ingenuity and cunning in the face of seemingly insurmountable challenges. His willingness to think outside the box and use unconventional means to win Atalanta's heart serves as a reminder that love knows no bounds and that sometimes, the greatest victories come from the most unexpected places.

Chapter 10: Reflections of Loves Solitude

Narcissus and Echo: A Lyrical Ode

Prologue

This beautiful ode is a retelling of the myth of Narcissus and Echo from Greek mythology.

In the realm where echoes sigh,
A lyrical ode to love's silent cry.
Of Narcissus and Echo, a tale untold,
In reflections of love, their hearts enfold.

Narcissus, ensnared by his own allure,
Echo's voice, a love so pure.
In still waters, Narcissus gazes,

Echo's yearning, like a gentle haze.

A nymph's plea, a lover's call,
Echo's heart, ensnared in thrall.
Yet Narcissus, lost in his own reflection,
Echo's love, a silent affection.

In deep reflections, their love does bloom,
Narcissus and Echo, in solitude's gloom.
A tale echoing through time's refrain,
In love's embrace, they remain.

So let this ode forever sing,
Of love's reflection, an eternal ring.
In the echoes of love's solitude,
Narcissus and Echo, their hearts renewed.

Musical composition

Reflective and ambient electronica with gentle piano, capturing the solitude and echo of Narcissus' self-love.

Am - C - G - Em (Repeat)

These chords are played in sequence and repeated throughout the arrangement.

Note: The myth of Narcissus and Echo unveils a tragic tale of self-love and unrequited echoes. In these lyrical verses, choral rendition, and epic retelling, we explore the reflective nature of love and the poignant solitude that accompanies it.

Narrative retelling

In the ancient woods of Greece, where the trees whispered secrets and the rivers murmured melodies, there lived a nymph named Echo. Blessed with a voice that could rival the sweetest songbirds and a spirit as free as the wind, Echo roamed the forests with a lightness in her step and a melody in her heart.

But Echo was not alone in the woods, for there also dwelled a young man named Narcissus, whose beauty was said to be unmatched by any mortal or deity. With hair like spun gold and eyes as blue as the summer sky, Narcissus wandered the forest with an air of arrogance, his heart untouched by the love of others.

One fateful day, as Echo roamed the forest in search of companionship, she encountered Narcissus by a crystal-clear pool. Enraptured by his beauty, she approached him with a song upon her lips, her heart overflowing with longing and desire.

But Narcissus, oblivious to Echo's presence, paid her no heed, his attention consumed by his own reflection in the water. Entranced by the image staring back at him, Narcissus fell deeply in love with the beautiful face he saw reflected in the pool, his heart consumed by a passion so fierce and all-consuming that it left no room for anyone else.

Heartbroken by Narcissus' rejection, Echo retreated into the shadows of the forest, her voice silenced by the pain of unrequited love. And as she faded into the depths of the woods, her voice became but an echo, a haunting reminder of the love she had lost.

Meanwhile, Narcissus remained by the pool, his gaze fixed upon his own reflection, unable to tear himself away from the beauty he saw before him. And as he gazed into the depths of the water, his love for himself grew ever stronger, until he could no longer bear to tear himself away from his own reflection.

And so, Narcissus remained by the pool for all eternity, his love unrequited and his heart forever trapped by the beauty he saw in himself. And as the years passed, the forest echoed with the haunting melody of Echo's voice, a poignant reminder of the tragedy that had unfolded in its midst.

In the end, the story of Narcissus and Echo serves as a cautionary tale of the dangers of vanity and self-absorption, and the tragic consequences of love unreciprocated. And though their tale may fade into legend with the passage of time, the echoes of their love will linger on in the hearts of all who hear their haunting melody.

Choral rendition

In ancient woods where whispers roam,
Echo, with voice like honeycomb,
And Narcissus, fair of face,
With arrogance, he roamed the space.

One day they met by crystal pool,
Echo sang, her heart so full,
But Narcissus, lost in his reflection,
Ignored her song, her sweet affection.

Enraptured by his own fair sight,
Narcissus fell, in love's delight,
His heart consumed by his own grace,
No room for Echo's loving embrace.

Heartbroken, Echo faded away,
Her voice now but an echo, they say,
While Narcissus, by the pool's edge,
Remained entranced, by his own pledge.

In love with himself, he stayed,
His reflection, his only aide,
Forever trapped, by beauty's snare,

In the ancient woods, a tale so rare.

Their story warns of vanity's cost,
Of love unreciprocated, lost,
And though time may fade their tale away,
Their echoes linger, night and day.

Reflections and insights

In the retelling of the myth of Narcissus and Echo, we are confronted with the timeless themes of love, vanity, and the consequences of obsession. Through the characters of Narcissus and Echo, we explore the complexities of human emotion, the longing for connection, the allure of beauty, and the pain of unrequited love.

Narcissus, with his obsession with his own reflection, symbolizes the dangers of vanity and self-absorption. His inability to see beyond himself and connect with others ultimately leads to his downfall, trapping him in a cycle of isolation and unfulfilled desire.

Echo, on the other hand, represents the yearning for connection and the pain of rejection. Her love for Narcissus goes unreciprocated, leaving her voice silenced and her spirit shattered. Yet, even in her despair, she serves as a poignant reminder of the power of love to transform and transcend.

Chapter 11: Cloak of Deceit

Hercules and Deianira: A Lyrical Ode

Prologue

This beautiful ode is a retelling of the myth of Hercules and Deianira from Greek mythology.

In realms where heroes tread,
A lyrical saga of love, in shadows spread.
Of Hercules and Deianira, bold and true,
In a cloak of deception, their tale imbued.

Hercules, in prowess and strength so grand,
Deianira, in love's gentle hand.
With centaur's blood and a cloak's cruel sting,

A hymn to love, with tragedy to bring.

In Nessus' deceit, a potion's dire brew,
Deianira's love, in agony grew.
The fatal garment of Hercules' guise,
A mythic narrative where darkness lies.

In depths of shadows, where sorrows reside,
Hercules and Deianira's love, denied.
A story of betrayal, in darkness steep,
A sung narrative of love's treacherous leap.

So let this tale forever resound,
Of love's demise, in shadows profound.
In the cloak of deceit, their fate entwined,
Hercules and Deianira, in sorrow's bind.

Musical composition

Tragic opera with powerful vocal performances and a sweeping orchestral arrangement, conveying the weight of deceit.

Fm - Db - Ab - Eb (Repeat)

These chords are played in sequence and repeated throughout the arrangement.

Note: The myth of Hercules and Deianira unfolds as a tale of love, betrayal, and the consequences of a cloak woven with deceit. In these lyrical verses, choral rendition, and epic retelling, we delve into the tragic saga of a hero and a queen whose love meets an untimely demise.

Narrative retelling

In the verdant hills of ancient Greece, where the sun kissed the earth and the air was thick with the scent of wildflowers, there lived a hero whose name echoed through the ages, Hercules, the son of Zeus and the mightiest of mortals.

Famed for his legendary strength and courage, Hercules roamed the land, vanquishing monsters and performing feats of valor that earned him the admiration of gods and mortals alike. But amidst his many triumphs, Hercules longed for a love that matched his own boundless spirit, a love that would stand the test of time and endure through all trials.

And so it was that Hercules encountered Deianira, a maiden of surpassing beauty and grace, whose heart was as pure as her spirit was kind. Enraptured by her beauty and captivated by her gentle spirit, Hercules knew that he had found the love he had been searching for, a love that would change the course of his destiny forever.

With the blessing of the gods, Hercules and Deianira were wed in a joyous ceremony, their hearts entwined in a bond that seemed unbreakable. But their happiness was short-lived, for soon after their marriage, Hercules was called upon to embark on yet another quest, one that would test his strength and resolve like never before.

For Hercules was tasked with defeating the fearsome centaur Nessus, whose vile deeds had brought suffering to the land. In a fierce battle that raged for days, Hercules emerged victorious, but not before Nessus had inflicted a fatal wound upon him with a poisoned arrow.

As Hercules lay dying, his strength fading with each passing moment, Nessus revealed a treacherous secret to Deianira, a poison that he claimed could restore Hercules to full health if applied to his clothing. Desperate to save her beloved husband, Deianira soaked a robe in the deadly potion and sent it to Hercules as a gift of love.

But tragically, the poison proved to be more potent than Deianira could have ever imagined. As Hercules donned the robe, the poison seeped into his skin, burning with a fiery agony that no mortal could endure. And in his final moments, Hercules realized the depth of Deianira's love and the terrible mistake that had cost him his life.

Heartbroken by the loss of her beloved husband, Deianira mourned for Hercules with a grief that knew no bounds. And though her love for him endured beyond the grave, she could never shake the guilt of her actions, knowing that her love had unwittingly led to his demise.

And so, the tale of Hercules and Deianira endures as a tragic reminder of the power of love and the consequences of our actions. For even the mightiest of heroes are not immune to the frailties of the human heart, and even the deepest of loves can lead to the greatest of sorrows.

Choral rendition

In ancient Greece's verdant hills,
Where sunlight kissed, and nature spills,
Lived Hercules, of strength untold,
A hero famed, with tales unfold.

Amidst his quests, he yearned to find,
A love to match his valiant mind,
And there he found, in Deianira's gaze,
A love to light his darkest days.

With gods' blessing, they were wed,
Their love a bond, no mortal tread,
But fate had plans, a test of might,
In battle fierce, 'gainst Nessus' might.

With poison's sting, his strength did wane,
As Deianira wept in pain,
To save her love, she sent a gift,
Unknowing of the fateful rift.

The robe she sent, soaked in deceit,
Brought Hercules to bended knees,
As poison's fire consumed his breath,

He faced his end, in painful death.

Heartbroken, Deianira wept,
For love's embrace, in sorrow slept,
Her actions, born of love's own fire,
Had cost her love, the ultimate desire.

Their tale, a reminder of love's might,
And the consequences of our plight,
For even heroes, strong and brave,
Can fall to love's unforgiving wave.

Reflections and insights

In the retelling of the myth of Hercules and Deianira, we are confronted with the complexities of love, sacrifice, and the consequences of our actions. Through the characters of Hercules and Deianira, we explore the depths of human emotion, the boundless depths of love, the agony of loss, and the weight of guilt and regret.

Hercules, with his unmatched strength and bravery, represents the epitome of heroism and valor. His quest for love leads him to Deianira, whose gentle spirit and devotion captivate his heart. Yet, even the mightiest of heroes are not immune to the vulnerabilities of the human heart, and Hercules ultimately meets his tragic end due to the unintended consequences of his actions.

Deianira, in turn, embodies the power of love and the lengths to which one will go to protect and save the ones they hold dear. Her decision to use the poison on Hercules' robe stems from a place of pure love and desperation, yet it ultimately leads to his demise and her own overwhelming guilt and sorrow. The tale of Hercules and Deianira serves as a timeless reminder of the fragility of the human condition and the enduring power of love to both uplift and devastate.

Chapter 12: Threads of Destiny

Theseus and Ariadne: A Lyrical Ode

Prologue

This beautiful ode is a retelling of the myth of Theseus and Ariadne from Greek mythology.

In the realm where destiny's tapestry unfurls,
A lyrical tribute to love that forever swirls.
Of Theseus and Ariadne, a saga so grand,
Within the loom of fate, their hearts firmly stand.

Theseus, gallant and daring, strides forth,
Ariadne, with stories yet to be told, stays north.
Through labyrinthine trials, a hero's plight,
Ariadne's devotion put to the test, alight.

Threads of love intertwine in the maze's chore,
Ariadne's gaze, a beacon, evermore.
Through the Minotaur's den, they tread,
In the web of destiny, their love widespread.

Ariadne's gift, a luminescent guide,
In labyrinthine nights, love's truest stride.
Amidst the maze of feelings, they prevail,
Theseus and Ariadne, love's epic tale.

So let this ode resound for all time,
Of love's triumph, in destiny's prime.
In threads of fate, their love does weave,
Theseus and Ariadne, hearts believe.

Musical composition

Romantic classical piece with elegant strings and woodwinds, weaving a musical tapestry of destiny.

Gmaj7 - Dmaj7 - Em7 - Cmaj7 (Repeat)

These chords are played in sequence and repeated throughout the arrangement.

Note: The myth of Theseus and Ariadne weaves a narrative of love, labyrinthine trials, and the threads of destiny that bind them together. In these lyrical verses, choral rendition, and epic retelling, we explore the labyrinth of emotions and the threads that guide a hero and a princess.

Narrative retelling

In the ancient city of Athens, where the marble columns gleamed in the sunlight and the sound of laughter filled the air, there lived a prince named Theseus. Bold and courageous, Theseus was known throughout the land for his bravery and cunning, his name whispered in awe by both friend and foe alike.

But despite his many triumphs, Theseus harbored a secret longing, a desire to prove himself worthy of his father's legacy and carve out his own destiny. And so, when the opportunity arose to embark on a quest to slay the dreaded Minotaur, a fearsome monster that dwelled in the heart of the labyrinth on the island of Crete, Theseus saw his chance to prove himself as a hero.

Accompanied by a band of brave warriors, Theseus set sail for Crete, determined to vanquish the beast and free the land from its terror. But little did he know that his fate would soon become entwined with that of a young princess named Ariadne, whose heart would become his greatest ally in the trials that lay ahead.

For Ariadne, daughter of King Minos, had grown weary of her father's cruelty and the darkness that had consumed their kingdom. Drawn to Theseus by a force she could not name, Ariadne pledged her aid to the brave prince, offering him a ball of golden thread to guide him through the labyrinth and a promise of love that would endure through all trials.

With Ariadne's guidance, Theseus ventured into the heart of the labyrinth, his heart filled with determination and his mind set on victory. And when he finally encountered the Minotaur, a fierce battle ensued, the clash of steel against scales echoing through the twisting corridors.

In the end, it was Theseus who emerged victorious, his courage and cunning proving greater than the fearsome beast that had terrorized the land. And as he emerged from the labyrinth, triumphant and unscathed, Theseus found himself face to face with Ariadne once more, her eyes shining with pride and admiration.

With the Minotaur defeated and the people of Crete freed from its tyranny, Theseus and Ariadne set sail for Athens together, their hearts filled with hope for a future filled with peace and prosperity. And though their journey would be fraught with challenges and obstacles, their love would endure as a beacon of light in the darkness, guiding them through the trials that lay ahead.

In the end, the tale of Theseus and Ariadne serves as a testament to the power of love to conquer even the greatest of challenges and the strength of the human spirit to overcome adversity. And though their story may fade into legend with the passage of time, the love of Theseus and Ariadne would endure as a timeless symbol of hope and resilience for generations to come.

Choral rendition

In Athens, where the sun kissed the stone,
Lived Prince Theseus, his legend known.
His heart longed for a quest to roam,
To carve his path, to find his home.

With courage bold, he set to sea,
To face the Minotaur, set Greece free.
But in that maze, fate intertwined,
With Ariadne, love to find.

Ariadne, weary of her father's reign,
Joined Theseus, her heart unchained.
With golden thread, their paths entwined,
Guiding him through the labyrinth's bind.

With Minotaur slain, their triumph soared,
Ariadne's love, Theseus adored.
Together they sailed, to Athens' shore,
Their love, a beacon forevermore.

Through trials and storms, they stood as one,
Their love, a tale beneath the sun.
Though legends fade and empires fall,

Their love endures, the greatest of all.

With courage bold, they faced their plight,
Their love a beacon, shining bright.
In the annals of history, their names entwined,
Theseus and Ariadne, love's legacy defined.

Reflections and insights

In the retelling of the myth of Theseus and Ariadne, we are immersed in a tale of courage, love, and the transformative power of human connection. Through the characters of Theseus and Ariadne, we explore the themes of bravery, loyalty, and the enduring strength of the human spirit.

Theseus, with his boldness and determination, represents the archetype of the hero on a quest for greatness. His journey to slay the Minotaur symbolizes the trials and challenges that we all face in our own lives, and his eventual victory serves as a testament to the power of courage and resilience.

Ariadne, on the other hand, embodies the power of love and the capacity for compassion to transcend boundaries and guide us through even the darkest of times. Her unwavering support and devotion to Theseus not only aid him in his quest but also serve as a source of inspiration and strength.

Chapter 13: Bloom of Eternal Beauty

Adonis and Aphrodite: A Lyrical Ode

Prologue

This beautiful ode is a retelling of the myth of Adonis and Aphrodite from Greek mythology.

In the garden where love's blossoms unfurl,
An ode to passion, in nature's whirl.
Of Adonis and Aphrodite, so fair,
In beauty's bloom, their love to share.

Mortal Adonis, embraced by earth's grace,
Aphrodite's ardor, a goddess' embrace.
In fields where beauty and sorrow blend,

Aphrodite wept, love's story penned.

A flower's bloom, where his essence spilled,
A hymn to love, with destiny filled.
In cycles eternal, love's dance beats,
Adonis and Aphrodite, in nature's sweet.

Through seasons' dance, love's spark ignites,
Adonis and Aphrodite, passion alights.
A tale of love, in nature's refrain,
In beauty's bloom, their hearts remain.

So let this ode resound, forever sing,
Of Adonis and Aphrodite, love's eternal spring.
In nature's embrace, their love survives,
A hymn to love, in blooms that thrive.

Musical composition

Enchanting harp and celestial choir, creating a celestial atmosphere that mirrors the eternal bloom of Adonis.

F - C/E - Dm - Bb (Repeat)

These chords are played in sequence and repeated throughout the arrangement.

Note: The myth of Adonis and Aphrodite unfolds as an ode to eternal beauty, passion, and the cyclical nature of life. In these lyrical verses, choral rendition, and epic retelling, we explore the love story of a mortal and the goddess of love, intertwined with the bloom of nature.

Narrative retelling

In the golden fields of ancient Greece, where the earth was rich with the scent of wildflowers and the air was alive with the songs of birds, there lived a young hunter named Adonis. With his handsome features and athletic prowess, Adonis was the epitome of youthful beauty, his presence stirring the hearts of all who beheld him.

But it was not just mortals who were captivated by Adonis' charms, for even the goddess Aphrodite, the embodiment of love and desire, found herself irresistibly drawn to the young hunter. Enraptured by his beauty, Aphrodite watched over Adonis from afar, her heart aching with a longing she could not name.

And so, one fateful day, Aphrodite descended from Mount Olympus to the mortal realm, disguised as a mortal woman, in hopes of winning Adonis' affections. Taking on the guise of a huntress, Aphrodite joined Adonis in the fields, her presence stirring something deep within his soul.

As they roamed the countryside together, Aphrodite and Adonis grew ever closer, their hearts intertwining in a love that burned with a passion as fierce as the sun. But their happiness was short-lived, for tragedy soon struck, shattering their idyllic romance.

For Adonis, drawn by the thrill of the hunt, ventured into the depths of the forest alone, unaware of the danger that lurked in its shadows. And as he faced off against a fierce boar, he was mortally wounded, his lifeblood staining the earth beneath him.

Hearing Adonis' cries of pain, Aphrodite rushed to his side, her heart breaking at the sight of her beloved lying wounded and helpless before her. With tears streaming down her face, Aphrodite cradled Adonis in her arms, her grief echoing through the heavens.

In the end, despite Aphrodite's best efforts to save him, Adonis succumbed to his injuries, his life slipping away like the fading light of day. And as he breathed his last breath, Aphrodite wept bitter tears, her heart shattered into a million pieces by the loss of her beloved.

In the aftermath of Adonis' death, the fields of Greece mourned his passing, the flowers wilting and the birds falling silent in their grief. And though Aphrodite's love for Adonis would endure for all eternity, their tragic romance would be forever immortalized as a poignant reminder of the fragility of life and the power of love to transcend even death itself.

Choral rendition

In fields of gold where wildflowers bloom,
A hunter roamed, dispelling gloom.
Adonis, fair, with youth's embrace,
Captured hearts with his charming grace.

Oh, Aphrodite, goddess divine,
With love's ardor, you did pine.
From Olympus heights to earthly plain,
You sought his love, but found only pain.

As mortal guise, you joined his chase,
In fields and forests, side by side you'd pace.
With each passing day, your love did grow,
But fate's cruel hand dealt a bitter blow.

Oh, Aphrodite, tears did flow,
As Adonis faced his final woe.
Mortal wounds stained the earth below,
Your love's embrace, lost to the shadow.

The fields wept, the birds fell still,
As Adonis lay, his spirit to fulfill.
In your arms, he breathed his last,

A love so true, now part of the past.

Oh, Aphrodite, mournful queen,
In heavens high, your cries were seen.
Though Adonis now rests above,
Your eternal love, a testament of love.

Reflections and insights

In the retelling of the myth of Adonis and Aphrodite, we are confronted with the timeless themes of love, beauty, and the inevitability of mortality. Through the characters of Adonis and Aphrodite, we explore the depths of human emotion, the ecstasy of love, the agony of loss, and the enduring legacy of passion.

Adonis, with his youthful vigor and radiant beauty, represents the fleeting nature of life and the vulnerability of mortal existence. His tragic death serves as a reminder of the fragility of human life and the inevitability of death, despite the fervent desires of the heart.

Aphrodite, on the other hand, embodies the power of love to transcend even the boundaries of life and death. Her undying devotion to Adonis, despite the inevitability of his demise, speaks to the timeless nature of love and its ability to endure through all trials and tribulations.

As we reflect on the story of Adonis and Aphrodite, may we be reminded of the bittersweet nature of love, the joy of its embrace, and the sorrow of its loss. And may we find solace in the knowledge that, though mortal life may be fleeting, the love we share with others has the power to transcend even the darkest of times.

Chapter 14: A Humble Union

Baucis and Philemon: A Lyrical Ode

Prologue

This beautiful ode is a retelling of the myth of Atalanta and Hippomenes from Greek mythology.

In a quaint and modest cottage there lies,
A lyrical ode of love under skies.
Baucis and Philemon, hearts entwined,
Their humble abode, love's treasure find.

Elderly souls, with love's flame aglow,
Their humble dwelling, a sacred bough.
In welcoming the divine, they find their grace,

Zeus and Hermes, love's eternal embrace.

A feast simple, hearts overflow,
In generosity, love's seeds sow.
A tribute to love, in every part,
Baucis and Philemon, love's humble heart.

Their cottage, touched by divine embrace,
A shrine to love, in their tender space.
Through ages, their love brightly shines,
A hymn to love, in every line.

In life's ebb and flow, their love's refrain,
Baucis and Philemon, love's steadfast chain.
A tale of simplicity, a bond so true,
A hymn to love, forever anew.

Musical composition

Folk-inspired acoustic musical ode with warm vocals, reflecting the humility and enduring love of Baucis and Philemon.

C - G - Am - F (Repeat)

These chords are played in sequence and repeated throughout the arrangement.

Note: The myth of Baucis and Philemon unveils a narrative of humility, hospitality, and enduring love. In these lyrical verses, choral rendition, and epic retelling, we explore the simple yet profound love story of an elderly couple and their unwavering bond.

Narrative retelling

In the ancient land of Phrygia, nestled among rolling hills and lush forests, there lived a humble couple named Baucis and Philemon. Though they possessed little in material wealth, their hearts overflowed with love and kindness, their home a sanctuary of warmth and hospitality.

Baucis and Philemon had lived many years together, their love growing deeper with each passing day, their bond unbreakable as the roots of the ancient oak tree that shaded their cottage. Despite their meager means, they found joy in each other's company, sharing simple pleasures and basking in the warmth of their enduring love.

One day, as Baucis and Philemon sat together beneath the shade of their beloved oak tree, they received an unexpected visit from two strangers, a man and a woman, whose faces shone with an otherworldly radiance. Though they appeared as ordinary travelers, Baucis and Philemon sensed that there was something special about their guests, something that stirred a sense of reverence within their hearts.

Moved by a deep sense of hospitality, Baucis and Philemon welcomed the strangers into their home, offering them the best of what they had, a humble meal of bread, cheese, and wine served on mismatched plates, but given with the warmth of genuine affection.

As they dined together, the strangers revealed their true identities, Zeus, the king of the gods, and his companion, Hermes, the messenger of the gods. Astonished and humbled by the presence of such divine beings, Baucis and Philemon bowed their heads in reverence, their hearts filled with awe and wonder.

Impressed by the couple's kindness and generosity, Zeus offered to grant them any wish they desired as a reward for their hospitality. But Baucis and Philemon, true to their humble nature, asked for nothing more than to remain together for all eternity, side by side, until the end of their days.

Touched by their selflessness, Zeus granted their wish, transforming their modest cottage into a magnificent temple and their ancient oak tree into a towering monument of marble and gold. And as the years passed, Baucis and Philemon remained together, their love enduring as steadfast as the roots of the oak tree that had sheltered them in their humble beginnings.

And when the time came for them to depart this world, Zeus honored their wish once more, transforming them into two intertwining trees, a mighty oak, and a graceful linden, forever bound together in an eternal embrace, their love immortalized for all time.

And so, the tale of Baucis and Philemon serves as a timeless reminder of the power of love and hospitality, and the enduring legacy of kindness in a world that is often filled with hardship and strife. For even in the humblest of circumstances, love has the power to transform lives and transcend even the boundaries of mortality.

Choral rendition

In the land of Phrygia, 'neath skies so fair,
Lived Baucis and Philemon, a devoted pair.
With humble hearts and love so true,
Their bond grew strong as the oak they knew.

Under the shade of their ancient tree,
They welcomed guests with hospitality.
Zeus and Hermes, divine and bright,
Graced their home one fateful night.

Offering bread, cheese, and wine,
Their kindness shone like a star's pure shine.
Impressed by their selfless grace,
Zeus granted them a special place.

Their wish was simple, yet profound,
To stay together, forever bound.
Their cottage turned to a temple grand,
Their love enduring across the land.

As time passed by, their love stood strong,
Like the roots of trees, ancient and long.
When their time on earth was through,

Zeus united them as trees anew.

Entwined forever, oak and linden,
Their love, a tale that will never find an endin'.
Baucis and Philemon, in their love so true,
A testament to kindness, for me and you.

Reflections and insights

In the retelling of the myth of Baucis and Philemon, we are presented with a profound meditation on the virtues of love, hospitality, and the enduring power of selflessness. Through the characters of Baucis and Philemon, we are reminded of the transformative impact of kindness and the boundless beauty of love that knows no bounds.

Baucis and Philemon embody the essence of hospitality, welcoming strangers with open arms and offering them the best of what they had, despite their own humble circumstances. Their selfless actions not only reflect the importance of generosity but also serve as a testament to the intrinsic goodness that resides within the human spirit.

The divine intervention of Zeus and Hermes underscores the universal significance of Baucis and Philemon's hospitality, elevating their humble abode to the status of a sacred sanctuary and immortalizing their love for eternity. Their unwavering devotion to each other, even in the face of adversity, speaks to the timeless power of love to transcend the limitations of mortal existence.

Chapter 15: A Kingdom in Flames

Aeneas and Dido: A Lyrical Ode

Prologue

This beautiful ode is a retelling of the myth of Aeneas and Dido from Greek mythology.

In Carthage's halls, a timeless ode unfolds,
Of Aeneas and Dido, their stories retold.
A Trojan hero, bound by fate's decree,
And Dido, a queen, lost in passion's sea.

Dido, consumed by love's sweet refrain,
Aeneas, duty-bound, amid joy and pain.
A kingdom forged in love's fervent blaze,
Yet fate's cruel hand ignites funeral days.

In Carthage's twilight, Trojan embers glow,
Aeneas torn 'twixt love's pull and duty's flow.
In the ashes of kingdoms, a tragic fame,
Their love consumed in passion's untamed flame.

Their saga resonates through history's scroll,
Aeneas and Dido, in love's eternal toll.
A kingdom ablaze, their destiny unfolds,
A hymn to love, amidst ashes cold.

Musical composition

Intense orchestral and choral arrangement with tragic undertones, capturing the kingdom's fiery demise.

Am - G - Em - F (Repeat)

These chords are played in sequence and repeated throughout the arrangement.

Note: The myth of Aeneas and Dido unfolds as a tale of passion, duty, and the tragic consequences of love. In these lyrical verses, choral rendition, and epic retelling, we explore the love story of a Trojan hero and a Carthaginian queen, set against the backdrop of destiny.

Narrative retelling

In the annals of ancient history, amidst the echoes of empires risen and fallen, there exists a tale of love's fervent blaze, a tale of Aeneas and Dido, whose hearts were bound by passion's fire amidst the ruins of kingdoms built and lost. As their story unfolds, it becomes an ode to the tumultuous dance of love and duty, where the flames of passion consume all in their path, leaving naught but ashes in their wake.

Aeneas, the valiant hero of Troy, wanders the earth in search of a new home, his destiny entwined with the fate of his people. In the ancient city of Carthage, he finds refuge and solace amidst the splendor of Queen Dido's court, her beauty and grace capturing his heart in a whirlwind of desire and longing.

Dido, a queen in her own right, finds herself drawn to the enigmatic hero from across the sea, his presence igniting a flame within her soul that burns with a fierce intensity. In the embrace of Aeneas, she finds solace from the burdens of rulership, her heart soaring amidst the passion and promise of their forbidden love.

But destiny, ever cruel and capricious, conspires to test their love in the most tragic of ways. As Aeneas's duty calls him away from Carthage to fulfil his destiny as the founder of Rome, Dido is left alone to contend with the agonizing torment of abandonment and betrayal.

In her despair, Dido's love turns to bitterness and rage, the flames of passion consuming her kingdom in a fiery inferno of destruction. As the walls of Carthage crumble and fall, so too does Dido's heart shatter into a thousand pieces, her love transformed into ashes amidst the ruins of her once-great empire.

In the annals of history, their tale remains etched in the sands of time, a tragic testament to the power of love to both elevate and destroy, to inspire greatness and bring about ruin. Aeneas and Dido, forever entwined in the echoes of the past, serve as a reminder of the perilous path of passion and the enduring legacy of love's kingdom in flames.

Choral rendition

In the age-old annals of time's grand sweep,
Amid empires' rise and fall, stories keep,
A tale of love, where Aeneas, valiant and bold,
And Dido, queen of Carthage, their tale unfold.

In Carthage's splendor, their paths entwine,
A bond ignited 'neath love's fervent sign.
Aeneas, Trojan hero, finds in Dido's grace,
A refuge from fate's harsh, relentless chase.

But duty calls, and destiny's decree,
Parts them, as Aeneas must sail the sea.
Left alone, Dido's heart is rent,
In anguish and despair, her love is spent.

Bitterness and rage consume her soul,
As flames of passion consume her whole.
Carthage, once grand, now lies in ruin,
Their love, like embers, no longer in tune.

Their story, a warning, for all to heed,
Of love's power, and how it can lead,
To heights of glory, or depths of woe,

In love's kingdom, where flames may grow.

In history's echo, their tale remains,
A cautionary note, amidst love's gains.
Aeneas and Dido, forever bound,
In love's eternal dance, their fate is found.

Reflections and insights

The myth of Aeneas and Dido unfolds as a tale of passion, duty, and the tragic consequences of love. In this retelling, we delve into the depths of their forbidden romance, immortalized amidst the ruins of empires built and lost. Through the intense orchestral and choral arrangement of our musical composition, we seek to capture the essence of their kingdom's fiery demise, a symphony of tragedy and triumph, passion, and destruction. As we pay homage to Aeneas and Dido in this timeless ode to love's fervent blaze, may their story serve as a cautionary tale of the perilous path of passion and the enduring legacy of love's kingdom in flames.

Chapter 16: Constellations of Love

Perseus and Andromeda: A Lyrical Ode

Prologue

This beautiful ode is a retelling of the myth of Perseus and Andromeda from Greek mythology.

In the starlit expanse, an ode unfolds,
Of Perseus and Andromeda, tales of old.
Heroic Perseus, his sword aglow,
Andromeda, in plight's shadow.

Through tempests wild and monsters dire,
Perseus rides on, fueled by love's fire.

Andromeda, bound by fate's decree,
A symphony of love across the sea.

In cosmic dance, their spirits entwine,
Perseus and Andromeda, a love divine.
A celestial narrative, writ in the sky,
A myth of love that will never die.

In constellations bright, their saga's told,
Perseus and Andromeda, stars of old.
A love that gleams in the cosmic dome,
A hymn to love, in every poem's tome.

Musical composition

Ethereal and cosmic ambient soundscape with electronic elements, echoing the celestial journey of Perseus and Andromeda.

Fm - Bbm - Eb - Ab (Repeat)

These chords are played in sequence and repeated throughout the arrangement.

Note: The myth of Perseus and Andromeda unfolds as a celestial ode, where love triumphs over monsters and stars align in a cosmic dance. In these lyrical verses, choral rendition, and epic retelling, we explore the love story of a hero and a princess, immortalized in constellations.

Narrative retelling

In the vast expanse of the cosmic tapestry, where stars twinkle like diamonds in the velvet sky, there exists a tale of love's celestial triumph, a tale of Perseus and Andromeda, whose spirits soar amidst the constellations, forever intertwined in the eternal dance of the heavens. As their story unfolds, it becomes an ode to the enduring power of love, where heroism and sacrifice illuminate the darkest corners of the universe.

Perseus, the valiant hero born of divine lineage, embarks on a perilous quest to save the princess Andromeda from the clutches of a monstrous sea serpent. Through stormy seas and treacherous waters, his courage blazes like a beacon in the night, his resolve unyielding in the face of insurmountable odds. With each stroke of his sword and each beat of his heart, he inches closer to his beloved, driven by a love that knows no bounds.

Andromeda, chained to the rocky cliffs as a sacrifice to appease the wrath of the gods, awaits her fate with a mixture of fear and hope. Yet, as the sea serpent looms ever closer, she finds solace in the knowledge that her hero will come to her rescue, his love a shining beacon amidst the darkness that threatens to consume her.

In a cosmic clash of titanic proportions, Perseus confronts the monstrous sea serpent, his sword flashing like a shooting star, as he battles against the forces of chaos and destruction. With each strike, he inches closer to victory, his determination fueled by the memory of his beloved Andromeda and the promise of a future filled with love and light.

As the sea serpent falls beneath Perseus's blade, Andromeda is freed from her chains, her heart soaring with gratitude and love for her brave hero. Together, they ascend to the heavens, their spirits mingling with the stars as they become immortalized in the constellations that adorn the night sky.

In the cosmic realm, their love knows no bounds, their spirits forever entwined in the celestial dance of the stars. Perseus and Andromeda become a beacon of hope and inspiration, their tale echoing through the ages as a testament to the power of love to conquer even the darkest of nights.

Choral rendition

In the vast expanse of the cosmic tapestry,
Where stars twinkle like diamonds in the velvet sky,
There exists a tale of love's celestial triumph,
Of Perseus and Andromeda, forever intertwined.

Their spirits soar amidst the constellations,
In the eternal dance of the heavens' creations,
An ode to love's enduring power,
Heroism and sacrifice in the darkest hour.

Perseus, the valiant hero of divine birth,
Embarks on a quest to save his love from the earth,
Through stormy seas and treacherous waters,
His courage shines like a beacon, never faltering.

Their spirits soar amidst the constellations,
In the eternal dance of the heavens' creations,
An ode to love's enduring power,
Heroism and sacrifice in the darkest hour.

Andromeda, chained to the rocky cliffs,
A sacrifice to appease the gods' tiffs,
Yet in her heart, there's hope's soft glow,

For Perseus, her hero, to rescue her from woe.

Their spirits soar amidst the constellations,
In the eternal dance of the heavens' creations,
An ode to love's enduring power,
Heroism and sacrifice in the darkest hour.

In a cosmic clash of titanic might,
Perseus faces the sea serpent's blight,
His sword flashing like a shooting star,
Against chaos and destruction, he'll spar.

Their spirits soar amidst the constellations,
In the eternal dance of the heavens' creations,
An ode to love's enduring power,
Heroism and sacrifice in the darkest hour.

As the sea serpent falls beneath his blade,
Andromeda is freed, no longer afraid,
Together they ascend, to the heavens' embrace,
Immortalized in stars, their love leaves its trace.

Their spirits soar amidst the constellations,
In the eternal dance of the heavens' creations,
An ode to love's enduring power,

Heroism and sacrifice in the darkest hour.

Reflections and insights

The myth of Perseus and Andromeda unfolds as a celestial ode, where love triumphs over monsters and stars align in a cosmic dance. In this retelling, we explore the boundless depths of love's enduring power, immortalized in the shimmering constellations that adorn the night sky. Through the ethereal and cosmic soundscape of our musical composition, we seek to capture the essence of their celestial journey, a cosmic odyssey where heroism and sacrifice illuminate the darkest corners of the universe. As we pay homage to Perseus and Andromeda in this timeless tale of love and valor, may their story serve as a reminder that even amidst the vastness of the cosmos, love will always find a way to shine bright and true, forever guiding us home.

Chapter 17: Melodic Metamorphosis

Pan and Syrinx: A Lyrical Ode

Prologue

This beautiful ode is a retelling of the myth of Pan and Syrinx from Greek mythology.

In the whispering breeze, their tale does unfold,
    Of Pan and Syrinx, their story told.
Pan, the rustic god, with his pipes in hand,
    Syrinx, a nymph, in nature's band.

Through the woodland glade, Pan gave chase,
    Syrinx fled, with a nymph's swift pace.
In the reeds she found her refuge true,
    A hymn to love, in nature's view.

Pan, in his sorrow, played his tune,
Syrinx's form, now reeds strewn.
A melody of love, in the wild's embrace,
A hymn to their bond, in nature's grace.

In the rustling reeds, their love remains,
Pan and Syrinx, in nature's plains.
A tale of metamorphosis, a love divine,
A hymn to their bond, in every line.

Musical composition

Lively and whimsical folk tune with woodwinds and rustic instruments, embodying the playful pursuit of Pan.

D - G - A - Em (Repeat).

These chords are played in sequence and repeated throughout the arrangement.

Note: The myth of Pan and Syrinx unfolds as a melodic ode, where love transforms into the rustling notes of reeds. In these lyrical verses, choral rendition, and epic retelling, we explore the tale of a rustic god and a nymph whose love undergoes a metamorphic dance.

Narrative retelling

Amidst the whispering reeds and rustling leaves of the ancient groves, there exists a tale of love's melodic metamorphosis, a tale woven into the very fabric of nature itself. It is the myth of Pan and Syrinx, a rustic god, and a nymph whose love transcends the boundaries of mortal and divine, immersing them in a symphony of passion and transformation.

Pan, the wild and untamed god of the countryside, roams the forests and meadows with boundless energy and irrepressible joy. His heart is captivated by the ethereal beauty of Syrinx, a nymph whose delicate form and graceful presence embody the essence of nature's splendor.

In his wild pursuit, Pan chases after Syrinx through the verdant glades and sun-dappled clearings, his laughter mingling with the song of the birds and the murmur of the streams. Yet, try as he might, he cannot capture the elusive nymph, whose heart belongs to the untamed wilderness that surrounds them.

As Pan's pursuit reaches a fevered pitch, Syrinx, in a desperate bid for escape, calls upon the spirits of the forest to aid her in her flight. In a moment of divine intervention, she is transformed into a cluster of reeds, her delicate form melding seamlessly with the rustling foliage.

Pan, crestfallen and bereft, arrives at the spot where Syrinx once stood, only to find himself surrounded by the haunting melody of the reeds. In that moment, he realizes that his beloved nymph has undergone a metamorphic transformation, her essence forever intertwined with the natural world she so dearly loved.

In the rustling reeds, Pan finds solace in the bittersweet strains of Syrinx's song, his lament mingling with the mournful melody of her reed-filled sighs. Though their love may have been transformed, it lives on in the melodic tapestry of the grove, where every whispering breeze and swaying branch carries echoes of their once-untamed passion.

Their tale becomes a hymn to love's enduring power, a testament to the boundless creativity of the natural world and the transformative force of passion and desire. As Pan and Syrinx remain forever entwined in the rustling reeds, their love becomes a timeless melody that resonates through the ages, reminding us of the enduring beauty of love's melodic metamorphosis.

Choral rendition

In the heart of ancient groves, where nature's whispers weave tales of old,

Lies a love story, rich and bold, of passion's symphony, untold.

Pan, the rustic god, with laughter free, roams the fields with boundless glee,

His heart captivated, wild and free, by Syrinx, nymph of mystery.

Through verdant glades and sunlit streams, Pan chases Syrinx, lost in dreams,

But her heart belongs to nature's themes, where love and wilderness gleam.

As Pan's pursuit grows wild and fierce, Syrinx, in fear, makes her pierce,

Calls upon nature's spirits near, to save her from fate's icy sneer.

In divine intervention's light, Syrinx transforms, out of sight,

Into reeds, her form takes flight, merging with the grove's delight.

Pan arrives, his heart laid bare, to find his love is no longer there,

Only the reeds, with melodies rare, whispering in the perfumed air.

In the rustling reeds, Pan hears her voice, his sorrow deep, his soul's choice,

For though she's gone, his heart's rejoice, in the echoes of love's sweet noise.

Their love transformed, yet ever true, in nature's embrace, they renew,

A symphony of passion, old and new, in the grove where dreams ensue.

So let the breeze and branches sway, as Pan and Syrinx forever play,

Their love, a melody that will stay, in the heart of the ancient grove's array.

Reflections and insights

The myth of Pan and Syrinx unfolds as a melodic ode, where love transforms into the rustling notes of reeds. In this retelling, we delve into the transformative power of passion and desire, immortalized in the bittersweet strains of their eternal song. Through the lively and whimsical folk tune of our musical composition, we seek to capture the essence of their playful pursuit and haunting lament, a symphony of love that echoes through the ancient groves and verdant glades of the natural world. As we pay homage to Pan and Syrinx in this timeless tale of melodic metamorphosis, may their story serve as a reminder of the enduring power of love to transcend the boundaries of mortal existence and find expression in the timeless rhythms of nature's eternal dance.

Chapter 18: A Swim Through Love's Depths

Leander and Hero: A Lyrical Ode

Prologue

This beautiful ode is a retelling of the myth of Leander and Hero from Greek mythology.

In moonlit waters, Leander's heart did soar,
Towards Hero's beacon, on distant shore.
Through crashing waves, love's current strong,
Their bond unbreakable, their connection long.

Hero's light, a guiding flame,
Leander's love, a call to claim.
Through turbulent seas, his stroke was true,
A hymn to love, in the ocean's blue.

Across the Hellespont, a lover's quest,
Leander and Hero, hearts abreast.
In each swim, a testament bold,
A love story written, in waters cold.

In the depths of night, their love did bloom,
Leander and Hero, dispelling gloom.
A swim through love's depths, a courageous feat,
A musical ode of devotion, forever sweet.

Musical composition

Atmospheric and aquatic soundscape with gentle waves and melodic strings, portraying the daring swim through love's depths.

C - G/B - Am - F (Repeat)

These chords are played in sequence and repeated throughout the arrangement.

Note: The myth of Leander and Hero unfolds as an ode to love's daring swim, where a hero crosses stormy seas to be with his beloved. In these lyrical verses, choral rendition, and epic retelling, we explore the love story of a young man and a priestess, separated by treacherous waters.

Narrative retelling

In the ancient waters of the Hellespont, where the sea meets the sky in an endless embrace, there exists a tale of love's daring swim, a tale of Leander and Hero, whose hearts were bound by the tumultuous currents of passion and fate. As their story unfolds, it becomes an ode to the depths of love, where courage and devotion propel them through the stormy seas of separation.

Leander, a young man of boundless courage and unwavering determination, is captivated by the ethereal beauty of Hero, a priestess whose radiant presence illuminates the shores of Sestos. Their love knows no bounds, transcending the mortal realm to bridge the gap between land and sea, heart and soul.

With each nightfall, Leander braves the treacherous waters of the Hellespont, guided by the beacon of Hero's love shining brightly from the shores of Abydos. Through crashing waves and howling winds, he swims with unyielding resolve. His strokes are fueled by the fire of devotion that burns within his heart.

Hero, ever vigilant upon the rocky cliffs of Abydos, watches with bated breath as Leander's figure emerges from the churning depths, a solitary beacon amidst the darkness of the night. Her heart swells with love and fear, knowing that with each stroke, her beloved risks his life for the sake of their forbidden union.

Their nightly swims become a testament to the power of love's enduring flame, a beacon that guides them through the darkest of nights and the fiercest of storms. In the depths of the sea, amidst the crashing waves and swirling currents, Leander and Hero find solace in each other's embrace, their passion transcending the barriers of time and tide.

But fate, ever capricious, conspires to test their love in the most cruel and tragic of ways. On a fateful night, amidst a tempestuous sea, Leander's strength falters, and he is swept beneath the waves, his desperate cries lost amidst the roar of the surf.

In the aftermath of tragedy, Hero's grief knows no bounds, her tears mingling with the salty spray of the sea as she searches in vain for her beloved amidst the wreckage of the storm. Yet, even in death, their love remains unbroken, an eternal bond that transcends the mortal realm and echoes through the depths of eternity.

Choral rendition

In the ancient waters of the Hellespont wide,
Where sea and sky in endless embrace abide,
Lies a tale of love's daring swim,
Of Leander and Hero, hearts brimming to the brim.

Leander, with courage boundless and bold,
Is captivated by Hero, radiant as gold.
Their love, a flame that knows no end,
Across land and sea, they transcend.

Each night, Leander takes to the waves,
Guided by Hero's love, a light that saves.
Through crashing waves and tempests fierce,
His strokes fueled by love, never to pierce.

Hero, on Abydos' rocky shore,
Watches Leander, her heart at the fore.
With love and fear, she awaits his sight,
As he braves the sea in the darkest night.

Their nightly swim, a testament true,
To love's enduring flame, tried and true.
In the depths of the sea, amidst storms wild,

Leander and Hero find solace, reconciled.

But fate, with its whims, tests their love's might,
On a night when tempests blot out the light.
Leander, swept beneath the waves' roar,
Is lost to Hero, forevermore.

In grief, Hero searches the storm-tossed sea,
But finds not her love, ne'er again to be.
Yet in death, their love knows no end,
An eternal bond, forever to transcend.

Reflections and insights

The myth of Leander and Hero unfolds as an ode to love's daring swim, where a young man crosses stormy seas to be with his beloved priestess. In this retelling, we delve into the depths of their passion and devotion, immortalized in the crashing waves and swirling currents of the Hellespont. Through the atmospheric soundscape and melodic strings of our musical composition, we seek to capture the essence of their journey, a courageous swim through love's depths, where the heart's beacon guides them through the darkest of nights and the fiercest of storms. As we pay homage to Leander and Hero in this timeless tale of love and loss, may their story serve as a reminder that true love knows no boundaries and can withstand even the most formidable of trials.

Chapter 19: Eternal Spring of Love

Apollo and Hyacinth: A Lyrical Ode

Prologue

This beautiful ode is a retelling of the myth of Apollo and Hyacinth from Greek mythology.

In meadows green, where wildflowers sway,
Apollo and Hyacinth spent their day.
The god of sun, the mortal fair,
Their love bloomed bright, beyond compare.

In friendly games, a tragic twist,
The discus flew, love's fate kissed.
From Hyacinth's blood, a flower springs,
A hymn to love, where sadness sings.

In fields of blooms, Hyacinth's grace,
Apollo's tears, a divine embrace.
Eternal spring, where love does grow,
A myth of love, in nature's flow.

In every flower, in every breeze,
Apollo and Hyacinth's love does seize.
A tale of beauty, a love so true,
A hymn to love, forever new.

Musical composition

Uplifting and classical piece with joyful melodies and bright orchestration, celebrating the eternal spring of Apollo and Hyacinth.

G - D - Em - C (Repeat)

These chords are played in sequence and repeated throughout the arrangement.

Note: The myth of Apollo and Hyacinth unfolds as an ode to eternal spring, where a tragic throw of a discus leads to everlasting love. In these lyrical verses, choral rendition, and epic retelling, we explore the love story of a god and a mortal youth, immortalized in nature's bloom.

Narrative retelling

In the sun-drenched realm of ancient myth, amidst the verdant fields and blooming meadows, there exists a tale of love and tragedy, a tale woven into the fabric of nature itself. It is the myth of Apollo and Hyacinth, a timeless ode to the eternal spring of love, immortalized in the beauty of the natural world.

The story begins with Apollo, the radiant god of the sun, whose golden chariot illuminates the heavens with celestial splendour. Drawn to the mortal realm by the allure of earthly beauty, Apollo encounters Hyacinth, a youth of surpassing loveliness whose presence captivates the god's heart with a divine fervour.

Their love blossoms amidst the fragrant blooms of the meadow, where Apollo and Hyacinth share moments of joy and laughter, their spirits entwined in a dance of eternal spring. Yet, fate's hand is cruel and capricious, and tragedy looms on the horizon, casting a shadow over their idyllic union.

In a moment of playful rivalry, Apollo and Hyacinth engage in a friendly contest of athleticism, hurling the discus with strength and skill. But as fate would have it, a tragic twist of destiny unfolds, a wayward throw, a fatal blow, and Hyacinth's life is cut short in the prime of youth.

From the blood spilled upon the earth, a flower emerges, its petals stained with the hues of sorrow and remembrance. It is a symbol of eternal love, a testament to the bond between god and mortal, immortalized in nature's eternal bloom.

Apollo, grief-stricken and inconsolable, mourns the loss of his beloved Hyacinth, his tears mingling with the dew of the morning as he cradles the flower in his hands. Yet, amidst the sorrow, there is solace in the eternal spring that surrounds them, a reminder that love endures beyond the bounds of mortal existence, flourishing in the everlasting cycle of life and rebirth.

In the fields of Elysium, where the flowers bloom eternal and the sun's rays dance upon the emerald grass, Apollo and Hyacinth find solace in each other's embrace, their love immortalized in the eternal spring that blooms in the heart of every lover and the soul of every poet.

Choral rendition

In the sun-drenched realm of ancient myth,
Amidst the verdant fields and blooming meadows,
There exists a tale of love and tragedy,
Woven into the fabric of nature's melody.

Oh Apollo and Hyacinth,
Their love immortalized in nature's mint,
A timeless ode to eternal spring,
In the hearts where love doth sing.

Apollo, radiant god of the sun,
Drawn to mortal realm, his heart undone,
Encounters Hyacinth, youth of grace,
In their love, the world finds its embrace.

Oh Apollo and Hyacinth,
Their love immortalized in nature's mint,
A timeless ode to eternal spring,
In the hearts where love doth sing.

But fate, she casts her cruel decree,
A friendly contest, ends tragically,
With a fatal blow, Hyacinth falls,

Leaving Apollo to mourn his thralls.

Oh Apollo and Hyacinth,
Their love immortalized in nature's mint,
A timeless ode to eternal spring,
In the hearts where love doth sing.

From Hyacinth's blood, a flower blooms,
A symbol of love in eternal gloom,
Apollo weeps, his sorrow deep,
But in their love, forever they'll keep.

Oh Apollo and Hyacinth,
Their love immortalized in nature's mint,
A timeless ode to eternal spring,
In the hearts where love doth sing.

In fields of Elysium, they find their rest,
In love's embrace, forever blessed,
For in every lover's heart, they reside,
In nature's bloom, their love shall abide.

Reflections and insights

The myth of Apollo and Hyacinth unfolds as a timeless ode to the eternal spring of love, where a tragic twist of fate leads to an everlasting bond between god and mortal. In this retelling, we explore the beauty of their fleeting romance, immortalized in the blooming meadows and verdant fields of ancient myth. Through the joyful melodies and bright orchestration of our musical composition, we celebrate the enduring power of love to transcend the boundaries of mortality and bloom eternal in the heart of nature's embrace. As we pay homage to Apollo and Hyacinth in this uplifting and classical piece, may their story serve as a reminder that even in the face of tragedy, love will always find a way to bloom in the eternal spring of the human spirit.

Chapter 20: Firey Celestial Descent

Phaeton and Clymene: A Lyrical Ode

Prologue

This beautiful ode is a retelling of the myth of Phaeton and Clymene from Greek mythology.

In the heavens high, where stars align,
Phaeton's ambition did brightly shine.
Clymene's worry, her son's bold plea,
A celestial journey, destiny to see.

In the chariot's reins, Phaeton's grip,
Clymene's prayers, her heart did skip.
Through fiery skies, a daring flight,

A hymn to love in celestial light.

Clymene's tears, in the starry night,
Phaeton's fall, a tragic sight.
A mortal's quest, a mother's pain,
A myth of love in the cosmic domain.

Through constellations, their story told,
Phaeton and Clymene, love's tale bold.
A journey through heavens, fiery descent,
A hymn to love, in celestial lament.

In the fiery blaze, a son's bold quest,
Phaeton and Clymene, love's fiery test.
A celestial descent, in flames so bright,
A myth of love in the cosmic light.

Musical composition

Epic and intense orchestral composition with fiery brass and percussion, capturing the celestial descent of Phaeton.

Dm - Gm - A - Dm (Repeat)

These chords are played in sequence and repeated throughout the arrangement.

Note: The myth of Phaeton and Clymene unfolds as a celestial ode, where a mortal's quest to drive the sun chariot ends in fiery descent. In these lyrical verses, choral rendition, and epic retelling, we explore the tragic tale of a youth's ambitious journey and the consequences of challenging celestial forces.

Narrative retelling

In the annals of ancient mythology, amidst the celestial tapestry woven by the Greeks, there exists a tale of ambition, love, and tragic consequence, a tale immortalized in the myth of Phaeton and Clymene. Written by various authors in antiquity, including Ovid in his Metamorphoses and Hyginus in his Fabulae, this myth has captivated generations with its fiery imagery and poignant lessons.

The story begins with Phaeton, the mortal son of Clymene, filled with a burning desire to prove his divine lineage as the offspring of the sun god, Helios. With fervent determination, he implores his mother to reveal the truth of his paternity, and upon learning of his divine heritage, he sets forth on a quest to drive the sun chariot across the heavens. His ambition knows no bounds, fuelled by youthful arrogance and an unyielding yearning to ascend to the heights of celestial glory.

As Phaeton embarks on his audacious journey, the heavens tremble with anticipation and trepidation. Guiding the sun chariot, he commands the fiery steeds with trembling hands, intoxicated by the power and majesty coursing through his veins. Yet, his mortal frame proves inadequate to contain the immense power of the celestial chariot, and as he struggles to maintain control, disaster looms on the horizon.

Clymene, watching from afar, is filled with a mother's anguish as she witnesses her son's reckless folly. Her heartache is palpable, her tears mingling with the celestial dew as she beseeches the gods to spare her beloved Phaeton from impending doom. But fate, immutable and unforgiving, cannot be swayed by mortal pleas, and the tragedy unfolds with inexorable certainty.

In a crescendo of fiery brilliance, Phaeton loses control of the sun chariot, hurtling towards the earth in a cataclysmic descent. The heavens are rent asunder by the searing blaze, illuminating the celestial realm with an infernal glow as Phaeton's mortal form is consumed by the flames of his own ambition.

Clymene, her cries echoing through the cosmos, mourns the loss of her son, a tragic reminder of the perils of unchecked hubris and the immutable laws of fate. The myth of Phaeton and Clymene endures as a cautionary tale, a testament to the folly of mortal ambition and the enduring power of love amidst the fiery crucible of destiny.

As the echoes of their celestial descent fade into the ether, their story remains etched in the firmament, a timeless ode to the fiery passions that drive mortals to reach for the stars, even at the risk of being consumed by their own desires.

Choral rendition

In the annals of ancient mythology,
Amidst the celestial tapestry, a prodigy,
A tale of ambition, love, and tragic end,
In the myth of Phaeton and Clymene, it extends.

Oh Phaeton and Clymene,
Their tale in myths, a fiery scene,
With lessons wrought in flames so bright,
Their journey echoes through the night.

Phaeton, son of Clymene fair,
Yearns to prove his lineage rare,
A quest to drive the sun chariot high,
In his heart, ambition's fiery sigh.

Oh Phaeton and Clymene,
Their tale in myths, a fiery scene,
With lessons wrought in flames so bright,
Their journey echoes through the night.

But mortal frame, ill-fit for celestial grace,
As Phaeton struggles, disaster to embrace,
Clymene weeps, her heart in despair,

As fate's cruel hand, lays its snare.

Oh Phaeton and Clymene,
Their tale in myths, a fiery scene,
With lessons wrought in flames so bright,
Their journey echoes through the night.

In fiery descent, Phaeton's pride,
Consumed by flames, fate cannot abide,
Clymene mourns, her son's demise,
A cautionary tale, 'neath starlit skies.

Oh Phaeton and Clymene,
Their tale in myths, a fiery scene,
With lessons wrought in flames so bright,
Their journey echoes through the night.

As their story fades into the void,
In celestial realms, their echoes buoyed,
A reminder to mortals, to reach for the stars,
But beware the flames, that leave only scars.

Reflections and insights

The myth of Phaeton and Clymene is a timeless testament to the folly of mortal ambition and the enduring power of love amidst the fiery crucible of destiny. In this retelling, we explore the tragic consequences of hubris and the immutable laws of fate, set against the backdrop of celestial splendour and mortal longing. Through the voices of ancient authors such as Ovid and Hyginus, we unravel the layers of this timeless tale, weaving a tapestry of passion, loss, and redemption that resonates across the ages. As we pay homage to Phaeton and Clymene in this fiery celestial descent, may their story serve as a solemn reminder of the dangers of unchecked ambition and the enduring strength of love in the face of cosmic adversity.

Conclusion

In closing, "Mythical Odes Across the Ages" serves as a lyrical journey through the timeless tales of love, passion, betrayal, and transformation woven into the fabric of human existence. From the tender embrace of romance to the fiery trials of adversity, each lyrical ode and sung rendition, within this collection seeks to capture the essence of the human experience as told through the lens of mythology.

As you turn the final page, may these verses linger in your thoughts like echoes of ancient melodies, reminding you of the enduring power of love to shape destinies and transcend the boundaries of time and space. May you find solace and inspiration in the eternal truths revealed within these mythical odes, and may they continue to resonate in your heart long after the last stanza has been sung.

Thank you for embarking on this poetic odyssey with me. Until we meet again, may your own journey be filled with love, beauty, and the magic of storytelling.

About the Author

Peta Oakes, known for her evocative storytelling under the Gaelic pen name Mac Dubhdara, is a poet whose verses traverse the realms of myth and imagination. In "Mythical Odes Across the Ages," Peta embarks on a poetic odyssey that delves into the timeless tales of love, betrayal, and transformation woven into the fabric of human existence.

From the tender melodies of "A Tapestry of Love" to the fiery descent of "Firey Celestial Descent," Peta's lyrical verses, choral renditions, and epic retellings resonate with the soul-stirring echoes of ancient myths and timeless romance. Each chapter is a symphony of emotions, inviting readers to immerse themselves in a world where mythical creatures and mortal hearts intertwine.

Through the graceful flight of "Constellations of Love" and the tragic fate of "Tragedy in Mulberry Red,"

Peta captures the essence of love in all its forms eternal, transcendent, and ever-renewing. With each lyrical ode and sung rendition, readers are transported to enchanted realms where the boundaries between reality and myth blur, and the mysteries of the human heart are laid bare.

Peta's poetry speaks to the universal longing for connection and understanding, drawing inspiration from the rich tapestry of mythologies and legends spanning the ages. As readers journey through the pages of "Mythical Odes Across the Ages," they are reminded of the enduring power of love to transform, heal, and transcend the boundaries of time and space.

Through her lyrical verses, Peta invites you to explore the depths of the soul and discover the magic that lies within the mythical realms explored within these lyrical odes and sung renditions.

www.ingramcontent.com/pod-product-compliance
Lightning Source LLC
Chambersburg PA
CBHW051547020426
42333CB00016B/2135